Upon the Temple Lot

The Church of Christ's Quest to Build the House of the Lord

BY R. JEAN ADDAMS

John Whitmer Books

Independence, Missouri

2010

Published by John Whitmer Books, Independence, Missouri

© 2010 by the John Whitmer Historical Association.

ISBN 1-934901-34-2
ISBN-13 978-1-934901-34-2

Cover design and typesetting by John Hamer.

Table of Contents

Acknowledgements

I express my appreciation to John Hamer, Alex Baugh, and Roland Sarratt for their assistance with the illustrations, and particular appreciation to Bill and Annette Curtis for, not only their help in providing many of the photographs and other illustrations, but for their constant encouragement and countless hours of help and assistance in my research on the subject matter. Likewise my thanks to Chris Jones for his encouragement and introductions.

Thanks also to Ronald E. Romig, former Community of Christ Archivist, Mark A. Scherer, Community of Christ Historian-Archivist, Barbara Bernauer, Community of Christ Assistant Archivist, and Rachael Meisinger, Community of Christ Librarian; Bill Slaughter, Mel Bashore, Jay Burrup, Michael Landon, and Ron Watt (ret.) of the LDS Church History Library; and the staffs of the University of Utah Special Collections, BYU Special Collections, and Utah State University Special Collections.

Finally, a special thanks for research assistance to William A. Sheldon, Roland L. Sarratt, Richard A. Wheaton, Geri Adams, and Harvey Seibel, Church of Christ (Temple Lot) officers and members, without whose help this story could not have been written.

R. Jean Addams

Dedication of Temple Lot, August 3, 1831, by Joseph Smith Jr. Others included: Sidney Rigdon, Edward Partridge, William W. Phelps, Oliver Cowdrey, Martin Harris, and Joseph Coe, ANNETTE CURTIS

Introduction

> There is not one who calls himself a Latter Day Saint that does not believe a temple is to be reared at Independence on the site of ground owned by the Church of Christ.

S O STATED THE EDITOR of the Church of Christ's newspaper the *Evening and Morning Star* in its July 1907 issue.[1] Twenty-six years later the editor of their re-named newspaper *Zion's Advocate* proclaimed: "Now after one hundred and two years have passed by, it is still the dream of all Mormons to see the erection of a beautiful temple on the Temple Lot."[2]

To the vast majority of the Restoration churches who claim their original basis on the revelations of Joseph Smith Jr. as the "Prophet of the Restoration," the Temple Lot in the Center Place

---

[1] John R. Haldeman, "An Important Report," *Evening and Morning Star* 8, no. 3 (July 1907): 1. In the late 1890s and early 1900s the *Evening and Morning Star* was the official newspaper of the Church of Christ (Temple Lot). It was published in Independence, Missouri. The name was derived from the name of the first newspaper of the original church published in the early 1830s, also in Independence, Missouri. The *Evening and Morning Star* replaced the *Searchlight* (first published in 1896 at Independence) in May 1900 as the official organ of the Church of Christ (Temple Lot). The *Evening and Morning Star* ceased publication in late 1916, perhaps due to the reduced membership of the church and/or expense. *Zion's Advocate* began publishing in May 1922 (at Independence) as the official newspaper of the church and has been continually published since its inception to the present time. The publishing of *Zion's Advocate* was moved to Port Huron, Michigan between June 1928 and April 1929.

[2] Walter L. Gates, "The Church of Christ and Jackson County: A Brief Historical Review," *Zion's Advocate* 10, no. 7 (July 1933): 103.

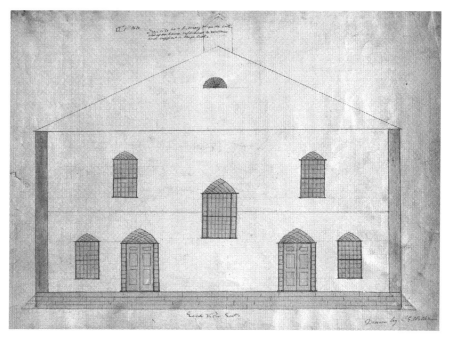

1833 plan for the proposed temple in Independence, Missouri, LDS CHURCH
HISTORY LIBRARY

Independence, Missouri, and the Jackson County Court House, 1836–1846,
engraving by Eigenthum d. Verleger, BILL AND ANNETTE CURTIS

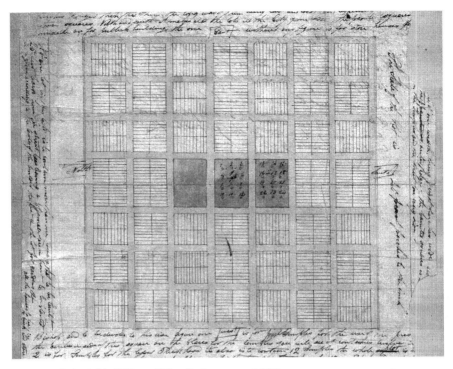

Joseph Smith's "City of Zion" plat map, 1833, LDS Church History Library

of Zion is a fundamental tenet.[3] The Temple Lot and its proposed temple or temples continue to be seen as crucial elements in preparing for the return of the saints to Independence, Missouri, and the eventual return of Christ.[4]

---

[3] Doctrine and Covenants, Section 42:35-36, Church of Jesus Christ of Latter-day Saints (Salt Lake City, Utah) (hereafter cited as [LDS D&C] and noted immediately following the quotation in the text); Doctrine and Covenants Section 42:10c, Reorganized Church of Jesus Christ of Latter Day Saints (Independence, Missouri) (hereafter cited as [RLDS D&C] and noted immediately following the quotation in the text). Note: For purposes of this article the Church of Jesus Christ of Latter-day Saints will hereafter be cited as the LDS Church and the Reorganized Church of Jesus Christ of Latter Day Saints will hereafter be cited as the RLDS Church. The April 2000 World Conference approved changing the church's name to the Community of Christ, effective April 6, 2001, while legally retaining its incorporation name.

[4] On June 24, 1833, Joseph Smith Jr. released his "plat" for the City of Zion, showing that there would be 24 temples at its center and giving his explanation for their use.

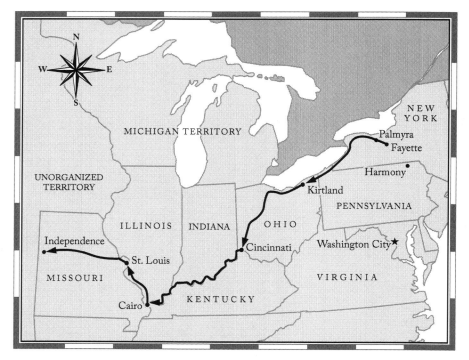

Route of the "Lamanite Mission" from the original center of the church in New York, through the later centers of Kirtland and Independence, JOHN HAMER

In February 1831, soon after Smith had relocated the church to the Kirtland, Ohio, area, he received a revelation which stated: "the time shall come when it shall be revealed unto you from on high, when the city of the New Jerusalem shall be prepared, that ye may be gather in one" and "it shall be revealed unto you in mine own due time where the New Jerusalem shall be built." (LDS D&C 42:62 and RLDS D&C 42:17b). To the members

---

See Joseph Smith Jr. et al., *History of the Church of Jesus Christ of Latter-day Saints,* ed., Brigham H. Roberts, 2nd ed., rev., 7 vols. (Salt Lake City: Deseret Book, 1971), 1:357-62 (hereafter cited as *History of the LDS Church*); Richard H. Jackson, "The City of Zion Plat," in S. Kent Brown, Donald Q. Cannon, and Richard H. Jackson, eds., *Historical Atlas of Mormonism* (New York: Simon and Schuster, 1994), 44-45; *Encyclopedia of Latter-day Saint History,* (Deseret Book Company: Salt Lake City, Utah, 2000), 211. Edited by Arnold K. Garr, Donald Q. Cannon and Richard O. Cowan.

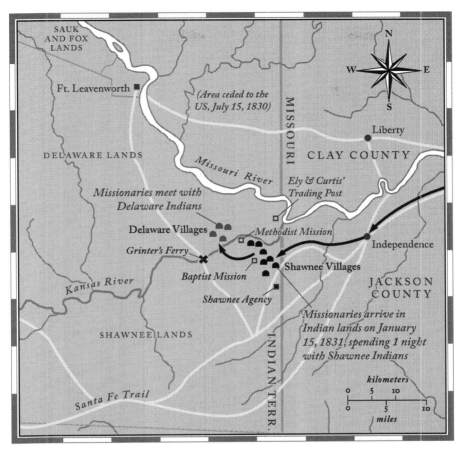

Route of the "Lamanite Mission" from the original center of the church in Missouri and the Indian Territory (now Kansas), JOHN HAMER

of the rapidly growing young church this announcement carried with it considerable excitement and a great sense of anticipation. Later, in June 1831, Smith was instructed through another revelation: "And thus you shall take your journey...unto the land of Missouri, unto the borders of the Lamanites." (LDS D&C 54:8 and RLDS D&C 54:2b) Smith and his companions left Kirtland soon thereafter and arrived in Independence, Jackson County, Missouri, in mid July 1831.[5] (RLDS D&C 54: Preface).

[5] *History of the LDS Church*, 1:189.

Shortly after his arrival, Smith announced the Lord's intention to make this location His chosen place for the gathering of His followers. In this revelation, the town of Independence, Missouri, was designated as "the center place; and a spot for the temple is lying westward, upon a lot which is not far from the court-house." (LDS D&C 57:1-3 and RLDS D&C 57:1a.-d.) In compliance to this revelation from the Lord, Joseph Smith Jr. and others dedicated this "spot for a temple" on August 3, 1831.[6]

Tragically, the members of the original church were driven "en masse" out of Jackson County, Missouri, in the fall of 1833. As a result of this forced exodus, the land claims of the church were lost and the plan to build a temple[7] on the dedicated "spot" was indefinitely postponed.

---

[6] Ibid., 1:196.

[7] As a result of the forced abandonment of the church's properties in Jackson County, Missouri (as well as property holdings of individual members of the church), these properties were either subsequently sold at a Sheriff's auction for failure to pay delinquent property taxes or were foreclosed upon by secondary owners who had not been paid under the terms of their respective contracts. It is further noted that in the early days of land acquisitions in Missouri it was illegal for a church to hold property as a separate entity; therefore, the 63.27 acre parcel (which included the dedicated temple lot) was held in the name of Edward Partridge (who was serving as the bishop of the church) rather than the name of the church. Jackson County, Property Records, Jones H. Flourney and Clara Flourney to Edward Partridge, December 19, 1831, B:1, Independence, Missouri. The legal description reads "63 and 43/160th acres in Section 3, Township 9, Range 32."

Granville Hedrick and the Emergence of the Church of Christ (Temple Lot)

I N THE AFTERMATH of the death of the Prophet Joseph Smith, and the exodus from Nauvoo in 1846, a significant number of Smith's followers remained behind or scattered to nearby states. Many of these followers aligned themselves with certain personalities who claimed to be successors to the mantle of Joseph Smith. However, in central Illinois there existed three branches of the early church that had remained generally aloof from the controversy swirling around these new claimants and their followers. These post 1844 branches (Eagle Creek, Half Moon Prairie, and Bloomington) were located in the vicinity of Woodford County, Illinois.[1]

---

[1] *Crow Creek Record, From Winter of 1852 to April 24, 1864,* Preface (hereafter cited as the *Crow Creek Record*). Transcribed and printed by the Church of Christ (Temple Lot), no date, Independence, Missouri.
    This is the title is as it appears in the current publication of the Church of Christ (Temple Lot) but is not so titled in the original document nor does the original include a "preface." The original document is titled *The Record and History of the Crow Creek Branch of the Church of Jesus Christ (of Latter day saints) which was organized on the 6th day of April A.D. 1830.* Note: There is no hyphen between "Latter" and "day." From 1852 to April 1864 minutes were taken by unnamed persons at meetings held at various places and at different times. It appears that at a later date the minutes or notes from these meetings were compiled into a single volume, again by an unnamed person. I make this deduction from the verb tenses used in the minutes. The compiler, when quoting the original record, generally used the past tense ("a meeting of the saints *was* held"). The original document was made available by the Church of Christ (Temple Lot) for microfilming to the Church of Jesus Christ of Latter-day Saints on October 4, 1977, in Independence, Missouri. Microfilm copies are available at the Church of Jesus Christ of Latter-day Saints, Family History Library, microfilm no.

Eagle Creek in Livingston County, Illinois, R. JEAN ADDAMS

By 1850 or 1851, the leaders of these independent branches apparently concluded to meet together as one branch. In time they referred to themselves as the Crow Creek branch of the Church of Jesus Christ (of Latter day Saints).[2] Later the Crow Creek branch dropped the "(of Latter day Saints)" and reverted to the original name of the mother church, i.e., the Church of

---

1,019,781, Salt Lake City, Utah, and the Community of Christ Library-Archives, Independence, Missouri.

 Note: In the preface, the scribe of the *Crow Creek Record* states that the Bloomington Branch (Illinois) was organized "in the early 30's" (1830s) and it is probable that the Half Moon Prairie and Eagle Creek branches were also organized in the late 1830s or early 1840s.

[2] There is no known record of this specific arrangement. The *Crow Creek Record* begins, as noted, in a previous footnote, in the year 1852. One can conclude from the dating of this document that the merger or amalgamation of the separate branches in central Illinois took place at, or before, this date. Note: The stream known as "Crow Creek" is located in the southern portion of Marshall County and is only a few miles from the homes of the Hedrick brothers and near to many of the other early members of the Church of Christ in Marshall and Woodford Counties.

Half Moon Prairie Park in Woodford County, Illinois, R. JEAN ADDAMS

Christ, as established on April 6, 1830, in Fayette, New York.[3]

[3] The name of the original church founded by Joseph Smith Jr. on April 6, 1830, at Fayette, New York, was recorded as the Church of Christ. (Also see the title page of the original 1830 edition of the Book of Mormon.) The name of the church was changed to the Church of the Latter Day Saints in 1834 during the Kirtland, Ohio period. It was not until 1838, when in a revelation to Joseph Smith at Far West, Missouri, that the name of the church was formalized as the Church of Jesus Christ of Latter Day Saints (LDS D&C 115:4). That name, i.e., Church of Jesus Christ of Latter Day Saints, was used thereafter with variations by the Church of Christ (Temple Lot) until the 1860s when the church voted to return to the 'original' name of 1830, i.e., the Church of Christ. However, the transition to the reinstated name took another thirty years before it became, more or less, standardized. The parenthetical enclosure (Temple Lot) was added later to differentiate it from other denominations of the same name and in particular the Church of Christ (Campbellites). The parenthetical enclosure (Temple Lot) is not part of the legal or official name of the church. Note: For purposes of this article the Church of Christ (Temple Lot) will be hereafter referred to and cited as the Church of Christ except where the parenthetical enclosure is part of a direct quote.

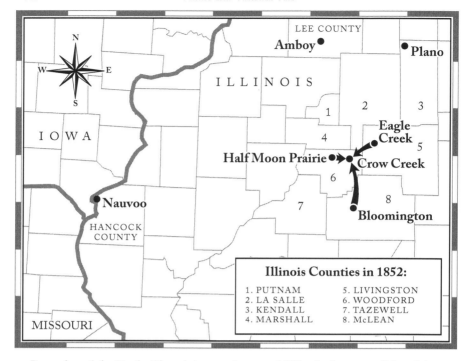

Branches of the Early Church in north central Illinois that consolidated into the Crow Creek branch in 1852, JOHN HAMER

Crow Creek in Marshall County, Illinois, R. JEAN ADDAMS

John H. Hedrick farm in Marshall County, near Crow Creek, R. JEAN ADDAMS

The first recorded meeting was held at the home of Granville Hedrick[4] (most likely the location of the Half Moon Prairie branch),[5] an elder in the original church, in Woodford County, in the winter of 1852.[6]

---

[4] Woodford County, Ill., Property Records, John H. and Elizabeth Ann Hedrick to Granville Hedrick, November 29, 1849, E:279; James B. and Minerva Martin, John H. Hedrick and Elizabeth Anne, and America and Mary Jane Hedrick to Granville Hedrick, February 25, 1850, E:280-81; and Jane Hedrick to Granville Hedrick, January 14, 1851, E:278-279, Eureka, Illinois. Granville Hedrick's farm was located approximately one mile directly west of the village of Washburn and within the Township of Casenovia, Woodford County, Illinois.

    Granville Hedrick was born in Clark City, Indiana, in 1814. He was converted to Mormonism between 1841 and 1843 and was baptized and ordained by Hervey Green (Official Church of Christ records indicate that he was baptized in 1843), probably in Washburn, Woodford County, Illinois, where Hedrick owned a large farm. *Truth Teller* 1, no. 2 (August 1864): 31. He had lived on the farm since his father, George Hedrick, purchased the property in 1834. Hedrick later acquired the property from his mother after the death of his father. Hedrick died at his home in Johnson County, Kansas, about 35 miles southwest of Independence, Missouri, in 1881, where he had purchased a section of land and relocated in 1874, rather than Jackson County, Missouri, as had been expected.

[5] *Woodford County History*, (Woodford County, Illinois: Woodford County Sesquicentennial History Committee, 1968), 20. Washburn was originally named Half Moon Prairie. The name comes from the early settlers who thought the shape of the prairie at this location looked like a "half moon."

[6] *Crow Creek Record*, 1. Also see: R. Jean Addams, "Reclaiming the Temple Lot in the Center Place of Zion," *Mormon Historical Studies* 7, nos. 1-2 (Spring/Fall 2006),

Several years later, on May 17, 1863, Granville Hedrick was ordained an apostle[7] by John E. Page.[8] Page, an apostle since

---

7-20.

[7] *Crow Creek Record*, 14. At this conference Page also ordained three other men apostles besides Granville Hedrick: David Judy, Adna C. Haldeman, and Jedediah Owen. All three men had been baptized in the early 1830s in north central Illinois. Also see: R. Jean Addams, "Reclaiming the Temple Lot in the Center Place of Zion," *Mormon Historical Studies* 7, nos. 1-2 (Spring/Fall 2006), 7-20.

David Judy was baptized and ordained an elder in Tazewell County, Illinois, in 1831 (Tazewell County adjoins Woodford County to the southwest). Judy was a farmer and a very early settler. He traveled with the church to Missouri in the late 1830s and, after the expulsion in 1838/39, he returned to his land holdings in Tazewell County. After Granville Hedrick's death in 1881 he became president of the Church of Christ. Interestingly, Judy never moved to Missouri and died in Tazewell County in 1886. Arrington, *Charles C Rich: Mormon General and Western Frontiersman*, 339; "More Testimony If Called For," *Truth Teller* 1, no. 2 (August 1864): 30-31; Bert C. Flint, *An Outline History of the Church of Christ* (Temple Lot) (Independence, Missouri: The Board of Publications, Church of Christ, 1953), 98 (hereafter cited as Flint, *An Outline History of the Church of Christ*).

Adna C. Haldeman was baptized in the original church in the early 1830s and, most likely, was an early leader of the Bloomington, Illinois, branch of the church (McLean County is located to the southeast of Woodford County), which dates from the early 1830s. Haldeman was skilled as a stone and monument mason and he and his family operated a thriving business for decades in Bloomington. He moved with his family to Independence, Missouri, in the late 1860s where he again established a business as a stone and monument mason. Haldeman died in 1881 and is buried in Independence, Missouri. "More Testimony If Called For," *Truth Teller* 1, no. 2 (August 1864): 30-31; Flint, *An Outline History of the Church of Christ*, 98.

Jedediah Owen was baptized in 1832 (probably in Tazewell County, Illinois). Owen moved with the saints to northern Missouri in the late 1830s. He was taken a prisoner following the surrender at Far West, Missouri, in early November of 1838. After his release he returned to farming in Marshall County (Marshall County is located to the immediate north of Woodford County). He made his first trip to Independence, Missouri, in 1865 and purchased a farm in advance of the main body of the church, which came in 1867-68. Owen died in 1881. Church of Christ Membership Record at Independence, Missouri, 1; "More Testimony If Called For," *Truth Teller* 1, no. 2 (August 1864): 30-31; Flint, *An Outline History of the Church of Christ*, 98.

[8] John E. Page had been baptized in August 1833 and ordained an elder in the original church in September 1833. His ordination to the office of apostle came in 1838 at Far West, Missouri. However, within a year and a half of the death of Joseph Smith, Page became disaffected with the leadership of Brigham Young, and was subsequently excommunicated. Brigham H. Roberts, *A Comprehensive History of the Church, Century One*, 6 vols. (Provo, Utah: Corporation of the Church of Jesus Christ of Latter-day Saints, 1965 printing), 2:431.

1838 in Joseph Smith's Quorum of the Twelve Apostles, had been a member of the Crow Creek branch since 1862.[9] Two months later on July 19, 1863, Hedrick was ordained by Page as the "Prophet, Seer, Revelator and Translator" of the church.[10]

In 1864, Granville Hedrick received a revelation which was promptly published in the church's newspaper the *Truth Teller*.[11] Granville claimed he was visited by an angel on April 24, 1864, who instructed him and his followers to "gather together upon the consecrated land which I have appointed and dedicated by My servant Joseph Smith...in Jackson County, state of Missouri." They were specifically told that "inasmuch as my church and people have been driven and scattered, therefore take counsel of me, your Lord and director, who says unto you: prepare yourselves and be ready against the appointed time which I have set and prepared for you, that you may return in the year A.D. 1867, which time the Lord, by your prayers and faithfulness in all things, will open and prepare a way before you that you may begin to gather at that time."[12]

Thus, the time was set for a gathering of these saints in 1867 to return and reclaim the Center Place of Zion or, more specifically, the Temple Lot and to fulfill the revelation given to Joseph

---

[9] *Crow Creek Record*, 12.

[10] Ibid., 15. Page stated that he was "mouth" for the Quorum of Apostles and that Judy, Haldeman, and Owen joined him in this ordinance. Also see, R. Jean Addams, "The Church of Christ (Temple Lot), Its Emergence, Struggles and Early Schisms," *Scattering of the Saints Schism within Mormonism*, edited by Newell G. Bringhurst and John C. Hamer (Independence, Missouri: John Whitmer Books, 2007), 206-223.

[11] The *Truth Teller* was the official monthly newspaper of the Church of Christ published between July 1864 and June 1865 at Bloomington, Illinois (Pantagraph Press). Publication was restarted in June 1868 at Independence, Missouri (two issues only — unknown press). Note: the name used in the masthead is the "Church of Jesus Christ (of Latter Day Saints"). Obviously, in spite of efforts to return to the original name of the church, i.e., the Church of Christ, the name by which the church identified itself in the publishing of its early newspapers (masthead and elsewhere) would continue to be used for thirty or more years. Likewise, in legal matters the Church of Christ often used (as its name) the Church of Jesus Christ (of Latter Day Saints) throughout the late 1800s.

[12] Granville Hedrick, "Revelation," *Truth Teller* 1, no. 1 (July 1864): 4.

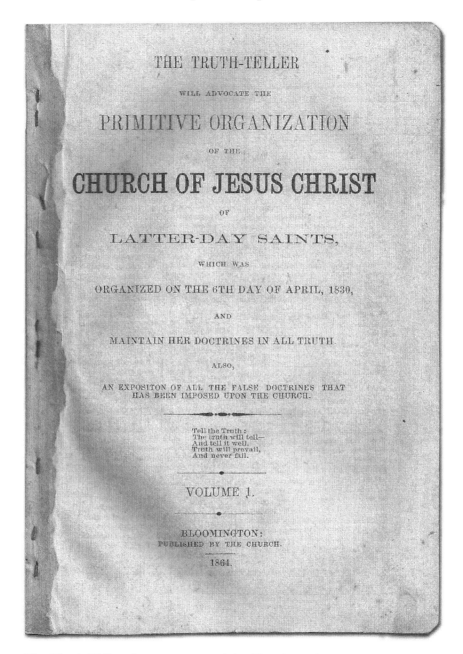

THE TRUTH-TELLER

WILL ADVOCATE THE

PRIMITIVE ORGANIZATION

OF THE

CHURCH OF JESUS CHRIST

OF

LATTER-DAY SAINTS,

WHICH WAS

ORGANIZED ON THE 6TH DAY OF APRIL, 1830,

AND

MAINTAIN HER DOCTRINES IN ALL TRUTH.

ALSO,

AN EXPOSITON OF ALL THE FALSE DOCTRINES THAT
HAS BEEN IMPOSED UPON THE CHURCH.

Tell the Truth:
The truth will tell—
And tell it well.
Truth will prevail,
And never fail.

VOLUME 1.

BLOOMINGTON:
PUBLISHED BY THE CHURCH.

1864.

The Truth-Teller, *first newspaper of the Church of Christ (Temple Lot), July 1864,* R. JEAN ADDAMS

Smith in July 1831. Among the diverse expressions of the Latter Day Saint movement, the Church of Christ or "Hedrickites" (as members of their church have been called historically) is unique in its early claim to a specific revelation to return as a church to Jackson County, Missouri, and to redeem or reclaim the Temple Lot in the Center Place of Zion.

In compliance to Hedrick's revelation, a vanguard of three families sold their farms and homes and moved to Independence, Missouri, in 1865 and 1866.[13] After the arrival of several additional families in early 1867, John H. Hedrick,[14] Granville's brother and the leader of the small vanguard party of 1865/1866, initiated the purchase of three lots in 1867 of the original temple property dedication site of 1831. Each lot was acquired separately for $250 each or a total of $750.[15] On November 8, 1869, Hedrick "quit-claimed" his three lots (Nos. 16, 20, and 21) to his brother Granville Hedrick as "President of the Church of Christ and as 'Trustee in Trust' for the Church of Christ."[16] No additional lots were acquired for several years.

[13] Elmer E. Long, "Return to Zion," *Zion's Advocate* 7, no. 17 (November 1930): 175-78.

[14] John H. Hedrick was a younger brother of Granville Hedrick. John's farm, while located in Marshall County, Illinois, was only 5 miles from Granville's property in Woodford County, Illinois. John H. Hedrick, baptized a member of the Church of Christ in 1856, was possibly the first Latter Day Saint to return to Jackson County, Missouri, since the expulsion of the Saints from Missouri in 1838–39. In the fall of 1865, only six months after the cessation of hostilities in the Civil War, he traveled to Jackson County, Missouri, and purchased a 245 acre farm near Independence. Jackson County, Property Records, James and Charlotte Pollock to John Hedrick, October 11, 1865, 43:615–16, Independence, Missouri. Church members John T. Clark and Jedediah Owen also made purchases of farms in April and July 1866 respectively. Simon and Nancy Walgamet to John T. Clark, April 4, 1866, 44:564–65; and Jessee and Eliza Taylor to Jedediah Owen, July 23, 1866, 46:405–6, Independence, Missouri.

[15] Jackson County, Property Records, Jacob Tindall to John Hedrick, August 22, 1867, 50:331-32 (lot 21); John Montgomery to John H. Hedrick, September 24, 1867, 50: 332 (lot 20); and George W. Buchanan to John H. Hedrick, December 12, 1867, 53:526–27 (lot 16), Independence, Missouri.

[16] Jackson County, Property Records, John Hedrick, quit-claimed three lots to Granville Hedrick, November 8, 1869, 73:1-2 (lots 16, 20, 21), Independence, Missouri.

Finally, however, on July 9, 1873, William Eaton,[17] one of the early members of the original church and an early participant in the Crow Creek branch, purchased lots Nos. 17, 18, 19 and 22 for the sum of $525.[18] He followed this acquisition with the purchase of lot No. 15 on March 7, 1874, for $200.[19] (Lot No. 15 is considered the dedication site for the temple).[20] On November 5, 1877, Eaton "quit-claimed" to Granville Hedrick, acting as Trustee in Trust for the Church of Christ, the five lots that he had acquired in 1873 and 1874.[21] At last, eight contiguous lots, which approximated 2½ acres and encompassing the dimensions of the site for the first temple, were now in the name of the Church of Christ.

---

[17] William Eaton joined the original church in the early 1840s. He was a farmer with considerable landholdings in Livingston County, Illinois (Livingston County is located to the east of Woodford County). After Eaton's first wife passed away, he married the widow (Mary) of John E. Page in the early 1870s before permanently residing in Independence, Missouri, in 1873 or 1874.

[18] Jackson County, Missouri, Property Records, Joseph C. and Mary Irwin to William Eaton, July 9, 1873, 104: 311 (lots 17, 18, 19, 22), Independence, Missouri.

[19] Jackson County, Missouri, Property Records, Maria McClanahan and Susan Nelson to William Eaton, March 7, 1874, 104:517 (lot 15), Independence, Missouri.

[20] Richard Price and Pamela Price, *The Temple of the Lord* (Independence, Missouri: Price Publishing Company, 1982), 73-85 (hereafter cited as Price and Price, *Temple of the Lord*). The Price's published the testimony of John Taylor (a member of the original church but not the 3rd president of the LDS Church), given in the Temple Lot Case. Taylor said: "the corner stone was up above the ground that marked the Temple, and I saw it myself with these eyes." The Price's included several testimonies dealing with the cornerstone on the temple lot. The cornerstone referred to was located on Lot 15 of the 1851 Maxwell-Woodson addition to the City of Independence.

[21] Jackson County, Property Records, William Eaton, quit-claimed five lots to Granville Hedrick, November 5, 1877, 115:452-54 (lots 15, 17, 18, 19, 22), Independence, Missouri.

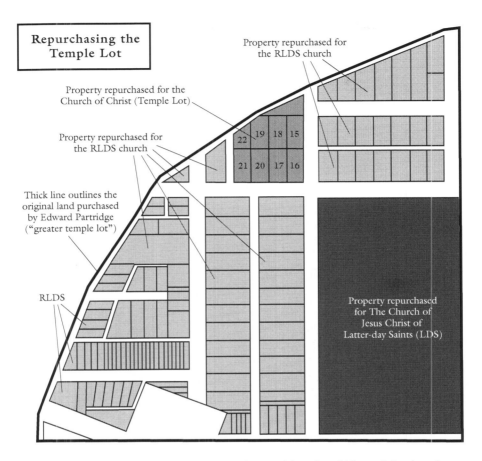

Temple property acquired by Edward Partridge, first bishop of the church, December 1831. Current owners of specific parcels identified, JOHN HAMER

Temple property acquired by Edward Partridge, first bishop of the church, December 1831. Current owners of specific parcels identified, JOHN HAMER

To Build a Temple

BETWEEN THE DATES of acquisitions of lots by John H. Hedrick and William Eaton, George D. Cole, a recent convert to the Church of Christ, recorded a magnificent dream regarding the construction of a temple on the sacred space known as the Temple Lot soon after his baptism in 1870.[1]

Two years later, Granville Hedrick received a revelation (1872) in which he was told:

> And as the building of an house unto the Lord in Independence, the Saints if they are faithful shall have power to accomplish it; but let it not be built after the manner of a church, but for a house of business for the building on the temple draweth nigh; therefore let the first house be a house for business, for store, for printing, and for counsel, and also for meeting and worshipping.[2]

Certainly this revelation, if not the Cole dream, or even the possibility of the death of John H. Hedrick in 1872, spurred on Eaton in his acquisition of the necessary remaining five lots.[3]

---

[1] George D. Cole, "Dream or Vision," *Zion's Advocate* 3, no. 10 (November 1926): 2 (rpt from *Evening and Morning Star* 17, no. 12 (March 1916.)

[2] John R. Haldeman, "An Important Action," *Searchlight* 3, no. 9 (October 1898): 261. As noted previously, the *Searchlight* was published by the Church of Christ (Temple Lot) at Independence, Missouri, beginning with the February 1896 issue. Monthly publication continued through March 1900. John R. Haldeman served as editor, first of the *Searchlight* and subsequently the *Evening and Morning Star*, until his death in December 1912. Haldeman was the son of early church member Adna C. Haldeman. Flint, *An Outline History of the Church of Christ*, 123.

[3] "Obituaries," *True Latter Day Saints' Herald* 19, no. 18 (September 15, 1872): 574. The *True Latter Day Saints' Herald* was first published in 1860 at Cincinnati, Ohio. Beginning in 1863 the paper was printed in Plano, Illinois. In January 1877 the

The reason for the significant time gap between Eaton's last lot purchase and his quit claim deed to Granville Hedrick is not known. Perhaps it was because Hedrick had moved to a farm in eastern Kansas and was not often in Independence or that the remaining desired lots were unavailable for purchase.[4]

Regardless, ten and twelve days respectively after Eaton's quit-claiming his lots to Granville Hedrick as the "Trustee in Trust" for the Church of Christ, the *St. Louis Globe-Democrat* and *Kansas City Times* carried an article titled: "A Mormon Temple for Missouri." The article stated that:

> The site for their Temple, has been re-purchased by the remnant of the Church which relocated here some years ago, and it is definitely asserted that the erection of the Temple will shortly be commenced. The lots have been unoccupied for the past forty-four years.[5]

This article was the first published announcement that a temple was to be built in Jackson County since the revelation to Joseph Smith Jr. in July 1831, forty-six years earlier.

Joseph Smith III, son of the Prophet Joseph Smith and president of the Reorganized Church of Jesus Christ of Latter Day Saints,[6] had announced in 1877 that those members who

name of the paper was changed to *Saints' Herald* and in 1881 the paper was relocated to Lamoni, Iowa. The paper was again relocated to Independence, Missouri, in 1920 and more recently the name has again been modified to the *Herald* (hereafter cited as the *Herald*). William Eaton may not have had the financial resources readily available to purchase the lots until 1873 because he had not liquidated his real estate holdings in Livingston County, Illinois, until 1873. In addition, there was the matter of settling the John E. Page estate, which, of course, involved Eaton's wife (and Page's widow), and himself as a lien holder (in the settlement of the estate). Apparently, Eaton did not permanently relocate to Independence, Missouri, until 1873 or 1874.

4 Johnson County, Property Records, Francis M. and Susie B. Black and David Waldo and William McCoy to Granville Hedrick, August 29, 1874, 29:62, Olathe, Kansas.

5 "A Mormon Temple for Missouri," *St. Louis Globe-Democrat* (*St. Louis, Missouri*), November 15, 1877, 1; "A Mormon Temple for Missouri," *Kansas City Times*, (*Kansas City, Missouri*), November 17, 1877, 2.

6 Joseph Smith III was the eldest surviving son of Joseph Smith Jr. and Emma Hale Smith. He was born in Kirtland, Ohio, on November 6, 1832. Smith was only eleven years old when his father was murdered at Carthage, Illinois. When Brigham Young

Illustration of the temple from Joseph Smith III's dream, COMMUNITY OF CHRIST LIBRARY-ARCHIVES

wished could "now" return to Jackson County.[7] (In 1864, at approximately the same time as Granville Hedrick's revelation, Smith had announced and published his "command" that the time was "not now" for any contemplated return of members of the RLDS Church to Jackson County, Missouri).[8] This

---

led the majority of the saints in the Nauvoo, Illinois, area west, young Joseph's mother and siblings stayed behind. Emma's family remained aloof from the claims of the many aspirants to the mantle of her husband. In the late 1850s, several individuals began to assimilate many of the Latter Day Saints that had remained in the Midwest. Certain of these individuals believed that Joseph Smith III should be the head of a "New Organization." In early 1860 Smith agreed and on April 6, 1860 (30 years to the day that his father had organized the original church), he was sustained as "President of the Church of Jesus Christ of Latter Day Saints." On February 5, 1873, in an effort to distinguish Joseph Smith III's church from Brigham Young's church of the same name, headquartered in Salt Lake City, Utah, the name was changed to the Reorganized Church of Jesus Christ of Latter Day Saints. Joseph Smith III presided over the RLDS Church for over 54 years. His death occurred in Independence, Missouri, on December 10, 1914.

[7] Joseph Smith III and Heman C. Smith, *The History of the Reorganized Church of Jesus Christ of Latter Day Saints*, 8 vols. (Lamoni, Iowa: Herald Publishing House, 1896) 4:166-67 and 3:709-14 (hereafter cited as the *History of the RLDS Church.*) Reprint (Independence, Missouri: Herald House, n.d.); *Herald* 27 (Plano, Illinois) (January 15, 1877).

[8] "The Truth Vindicated — No.1: 'Tossed to and Fro,'" *Herald* 6, no. 4 (August 15, 1864): 49.

commenced a gradual movement of RLDS members to the Independence area over the next 40 years. The announcement that same year that the Church of Christ was to soon build a temple could not have been well received.

Within eighteen months of this announcement by the Church of Christ, Joseph Smith III revealed in the June 1, 1878, issue of *Saints' Herald*, his spiritual vision of the temple on the sacred Temple Lot in Independence, Missouri. This announcement, it is presumed, caused great excitement and exuberance among members of the RLDS Church. However, it may have caused even more provocation and anguish among the local members of the Church of Christ living in the Independence area. The vision as described was later drawn by artist Ernest Webbe and published.[9]

[9] Joseph Smith III, "The House of the Lord, as Seen in Vision," *Herald* 25, no. 11 (June 1, 1878): 161–63. This revelation pronounced by Joseph Smith III is also included as a chapter in: Alvin Knisley, complier, *Infallible Proofs* (Independence: Herald Publishing House, 1930), 71-78 (rpt by Price Publishing Company, Independence, 1988). The citing used in the chapter is *Saints Herald*, April 15, 1878, which is in error. The Joseph Smith III "Temple Vision" is also included in "The Temple," Zion's Warning 3 (October 1972): 8 (a reproduction of the painting by Webbe is also shown), Special Collections, J. Willard Marriott Library, University of Utah, Salt Lake City, Utah.

A Meeting House to Precede the Temple

C ERTAINLY WITH THE Hedrick revelation of 1872, and perhaps
before, the members of the Church of Christ wanted to
build a meeting house or a place of worship on a small portion of
the property they owned in Independence. While the revelation,
previously cited, stated that the house had many purposes it
had specifically mentioned that it should be for "meeting and
worshipping."[1] The only enhancement of their property prior to
the construction of their first meeting house was the planting of
trees on the lot in 1883.[2] In the years following the departure of
the original church from Independence in the fall of 1833, the
local population had stripped the timber from the property.[3]

---

[1] John R. Haldeman, "An Important Action," *Searchlight* 3, no. 9 (October 1898):
261.

[2] *The Temple Lot Case* (Lamoni, Iowa: Herald Publishing House, 1893). Reprinted by
Price Publishing Company (Independence, Missouri, 2003), 175-76. Original title:
*Complainant's Abstract of Pleading and Evidence, In the Circuit Court of the United
States, Western District of Missouri, Western Division, at Kansas City: The Reorganized
Church of Jesus Christ of Latter Day Saints, Complainant, vs. The Church of Christ at
Independence, Missouri.*

[3] Price and Price, *Temple of the Lord*, 82. In his description of the Temple Lot, Orson
Pratt stated: "We commenced to lay the foundation of a temple about three quarters of
a mile from Independence, Jackson County, Missouri. It was then (1831) a wilderness,
with large trees on the temple block. I visited that place 47 years afterwards, namely
a year ago last September, and not a tree was to be found on that temple block—not
so much as a stump." Orson Pratt, *Journal of Discourses*, 26 vols. (Liverpool: Franklin
D. Richards, 1855–1866), 24:24.

Earliest known photo of the Church of Christ (Temple Lot) 1889 meetinghouse with several members gathered in front, BILL CURTIS

Official action to build a house of worship finally took place at the annual conference of the Church of Christ on April 7, 1884.[4] However, it was not until April 6, 1887, that a committee was appointed to "superintend the building of a house of worship to locate the same on [the] Temple grounds"[5] by conference vote of the members. The building was completed in 1889.[6] It was small in size, only 16 feet by 25 feet.[7]

Tragically, the little church was torched by an arsonist in 1898.[8] A new and much larger structure was commenced that

[4] Church Record (Independence, Missouri: Church of Christ), 65, cited by Flint, *An Outline History of the Church of Christ*, 114-15.

[5] Ibid., 114-15.

[6] Ibid., 115-16.

[7] Richard A. Wheaton, Temple Lot Plat (from plat used in 1890's Law Suit), plotted by Richard A. Wheaton, P. E., August 1999 (from Temple Plans, Photo Interpretation, Other Surveys, and Records). Copy courteously provided to author by Richard A. Wheaton.

[8] "Mormon Temple is Burned: Crank sets Fire to a Church at Independence," *Kansas City Times*, September 6, 1898, 6 ("W. D. C. Pattyson, who thinks himself an agent of the Lord, applies a torch to the building — gives himself up, confesses the deed

Members gathered at the south side of the Church of Christ (Temple Lot) 1889 meetinghouse, CHURCH OF CHRIST (TEMPLE LOT)

same year and completed and dedicated on April 6, 1902.[9] And, as had been the case with the first church constructed on the temple site, it was built as a prerequisite or a prelude to the construction of a temple in accordance to the Hedrick revelation of 1872.[10]

---

and makes a statement explaining his reason for his action); John R. Haldeman, "Our Meeting House Burned," *Searchlight* 3, no. 8 (September 1898): 254-55.

[9] John R. Haldeman, "Invitation Renewed," *Evening and Morning Star* 2, no. 11 (March 15, 1902): 3 and John R. Haldeman, "The Dedication," *Evening and Morning Star* 2, no. 12 (April 1902): 3. Flint, *An Outline History of the Church of Christ*, 127. A committee was appointed in September 1898 and conference action "to approve" occurred in October 1898. John R. Haldeman, "An Important Action," *Searchlight* 3, no. 9 (September 1898), 260-64. The cost of the new building was approximately $1800. John R. Haldeman, "The Dedication," *Evening and Morning Star* 2, no. 12 (April 1902), 3.

[10] John R. Haldeman, "An Important Action," *Searchlight* 3, no. 9 (October 1898): 260-64.

Church of Christ (Temple Lot) 1889 meetinghouse shortly after September 4, 1898, when fire destroyed the structure, RICHARD A. WHEATON

The Temple Lot Case — A Contest over Sacred Space

O N MAY 22, 1884, only six weeks after the Church of Christ conference voted to "fast and pray for a special favor of the Lord in reference to building of a house of worship on the Temple Lots,"[1] Alexander H. Smith[2] (brother of President Joseph Smith III) wrote to Edmund L. Kelley[3] (presiding bishop of the RLDS Church) and asked him "what think you of buying the Temple lot here? We can now buy it for just the cost of purchase, back taxes, and cost of improvements. $1800.00. The Hedricites [sic] wants [sic] us to buy it."[4] Continuing, he stated:

---

[1] Church Record (Independence, Missouri: Church of Christ), 57 (cited by Flint, *An Outline History of the Church of Christ*, 114).

[2] Alexander Hale Smith was born June 2, 1838, at Far West, Missouri, the son of Joseph and Emma Hale Smith. In 1873 he was ordained an apostle in the RLDS Church and in 1897 sustained a counselor in the First Presidency of his brother, Joseph Smith III, President of the RLDS Church. Smith was simultaneously ordained as the Patriarch/Evangelist to the church. In 1902 he was released from the First Presidency but continued in his responsibilities as the Patriarch/Evangelist. Smith died August 12, 1909.

[3] Edmund L. Kelley was born November 17, 1844, at Vienna, Illinois. Kelley was baptized a member of the RLDS Church at age 19 in 1864. He graduated from the University of Iowa, School of Law, in 1872. In 1882 he was ordained an elder and called as a counselor to the Presiding Bishop of the RLDS Church. Kelley was designated to represent the RLDS Church in the "Temple Lot Case." He was ordained as the Presiding Bishop in 1891 and in 1897 he also assumed the position of Counselor to President Joseph Smith III. Kelley was released as Presiding Bishop in 1916 and died May 23, 1930.

[4] Alexander H. Smith, Letter to Bishop Edmund L. Kelley, May 22, 1884, Alexander H. Smith Letters, P16, F6, Community of Christ Library-Archives.

Richard E. Hill of the Church of Christ (Temple Lot)

"I favor buying it. Think of it and talk to William and Blakeslee. Dont [sic] talk to any one else. We or the present holders do not want it generally known until the sale is made. Write me soon and let me know what you think of the project."[5] One can only speculate as to why someone from the Church of Christ would ever suggest such a transaction.

Obviously nothing developed regarding this potential ownership change. However, a conference of elders of these two churches did meet in 1885 "to confer… in a friendly discussion of the differences, real or supposed, existing between the two bodies."[6] Unfortunately, the "mending" that may have taken place in 1885 did not last long due to Smith's preoccupation with the physical possession of the Temple Lot.

[5] Ibid.

[6] Mary Audentia Smith Anderson, ed., *Memoirs of Joseph Smith III (1832–1914)*, photo-reprint edition, Richard P. Howard, ed. (Independence, Missouri: Herald Publishing House, 1979), 314 (hereafter cited as *Memoirs of Joseph Smith III*). The Anderson edition was serialized in the *Saints' Herald* (November 6, 1934, to July 31, 1937); Flint, *An Outline History of the Church of Christ*, 117.

*View of the Temple Lot showing Church of Christ (Temple Lot) 1889 church
and RLDS Stone Church, ca. 1890s,* BILL CURTIS

This preoccupation resulted in filing in the local court on June 11, 1887, by the RLDS Church, a Notice to Quit Possession against the Church of Christ.[7] Their claim stated that the 2½ acres "owned" by the Church of Christ should be relinquished to the rightful owner/successor of the original "trust" (created when Edward Partridge purchased the original 63¼ acres for the church in December 1831)[8] and that it, the Reorganized

---

[7] *Notice to Quit Possession,* "To Richard Hill, and all whom it may concern:-- You are hereby notified that the Reorganized Church of Jesus Christ of Latter Day Saints requires of you the possession of the premises known as the "Temple Lot," In Independence, Jackson County, and State of Missouri," G. A. Blakeslee, by Attorney, Bishop and Trustee for the Reorganized Church of Jesus Christ of Latter Day Saints," June 11, 1887, Independence, Missouri. This document was included in the Temple Lot Case as Exhibit 24. See also *The Temple Lot Case,* 247-48. The first printing did not include the "Decision of John F. Philips," who presided in U. S. District Court, Kansas City, Missouri, hearing of the Temple Lot Case inasmuch as the decision of his court was not handed down until March 3, 1894. The "Decision" was also printed by Herald Publishing House. Price Publishing Company, Independence, Missouri, has briefly summarized the decision of the U. S. Court of Appeals, which reversed Judge Philips, on the last page of the reprint.

[8] Jackson County, Property Records, B:1, Independence, Missouri. The exact date of the purchase is noted in the records: "Jones H. Flourney and Clara, his wife...to Edward Partridge, 63 and 43/160th acres in Section 3, Township 9, Range 32...dated December 19, 1831.

Church of Jesus Christ of Latter Day Saints, was, indeed, the rightful owner. Obviously, the ownership and possession of the sacred Temple Lot and its intended purpose, i.e., building the House of the Lord, had become a major point of contention. The Church of Christ, to no one's surprise, did not acquiesce to this threat. It was after this legal filing that the Church of Christ began construction of their first meeting house on the Temple Lot.[9]

After an interlude of approximately four years, the RLDS Church filed, in August 1891, a Bill of Equity in the U.S. District Court in Kansas City, Missouri, against the Church of Christ.[10] This action, and the entangled litigation that followed, is known

[9] Flint, *An Outline History of the Church of Christ,* 114-16. For twenty years, the church had planned to build a chapel, but the plans had never advanced beyond discussion. No doubt having heard of the RLDS planned action, the Church of Christ's April 1887 conference appointed "a committee of three…to superintend the building of a house of worship and to locate the same on the temple grounds." Construction began sometime thereafter (date is unknown) and the small building (16 feet x 25 feet) was completed at a cost of $377.41 before October 5, 1889, when the Church of Christ discharged the committee. From the RLDS Church leaders' point of view, this was an act of overt defiance of their "Notice to Quit Possession." See also Church Record (Independence, Missouri: Church of Christ), 65, quoted in Flint, *An Outline History of the Church of Christ,* 114-15.

[10] The Reorganized Church of Jesus Christ of Latter Day Saints, Complainant, vs. The Church of Christ At Independence, Missouri: Richard Hill, Trustee; [et al.], Bill of Equity, U.S. Circuit Court, Western Missouri District, Kansas City, August 6, 1891. Typescript copies of the Temple Lot Case can be researched at various locations including the following: Community of Christ Library-Archives, Independence, Missouri; Kansas City Missouri Public Library, Kansas City, Missouri; Church History Library, Salt Lake City, Utah. See also Ronald E. Romig, "The Temple Lot Suit after 100 Years," *John Whitmer Historical Association Journal* 12 (1992) 3-15, and Paul E. Reimann, *The Reorganized Church and the Civil Courts* (Salt Lake City: Utah Printing Company, 1961), 149-64. For information on the appeal of the initial decision see: The Church of Christ, [et al.], vs. The Reorganized Church of Jesus Christ of Latter Day Saints, U.S. Circuit Court of Appeals, Eighth Circuit, St. Louis, Mo., September 30, 1894 (70 Fed 179.), 188-89; "Judge Philip's Decision Reversed in the U. S. Court of Appeals," *Deseret Evening News,* September 30, 1895, and *The Church of Christ, et al., vs. The Reorganized Church of Jesus Christ of Latter Day Saints, U.S. Circuit Court of Appeals, Eighth Circuit, St. Louis, Mo., September 30, 1894 (71 Fed 250).* The second citing is a request to the court for a "rehearing" which was dismissed and thus set the stage for an appeal by the RLDS Church to the U. S. Supreme Court. Note: "laches" means "negligence in the observance of a duty or opportunity."

*View of the Temple Lot to the south, probably taken from a window in the
RLDS Stone Church, ca 1890s,* COMMUNITY OF CHRIST LIBRARY-ARCHIVES

historically as the Temple Lot Case. It occupied the attention
of both organizations' efforts for the next 4½ years. In January
1896, the U.S. Supreme Court refused to hear an appeal from
the RLDS Church.[11] In simple terms, this meant that nothing
had changed, i.e., the Church of Christ retained their property
as purchased by John H. Hedrick and William Eaton between
1867 and 1874 and later quit-claimed by them to Granville

---

[11] U.S. Supreme Court, Washington, D. C., June 27, 1896 (*163 U.S. 681.*); See also
R. Jean Addams, "The Church of Christ (Temple Lot), Its Emergence, Struggles and
Early Schisms," *Scattering of the Saints Schism within Mormonism,* edited by Newell
G. Bringhurst and John C. Hamer (Independence, Missouri: John Whitmer Books,
2007), 215. The decision reads as follows: "the members of the Reorganized church
have acquiesced too long in assertion of adverse right to the property in controversy
to be now heard to complain." The court concluded its decision by stating: "Under
these circumstances, we think that laches is a good and sufficient defense to the
action."

Hedrick as "Trustee-in-Trust" for the Church of Christ in 1869 and 1877 respectfully.[12]

Within days of the Supreme Court decision, the Church of Christ published its first newspaper since 1868. It was known as the *Searchlight*.[13] In its first issue of February 1, 1896, the editor stated:

> While the "Hedrickites" feel to rejoice that the Almighty has seen fit to allow them to remain in possession, still they regard the property as belonging to the Lord and will be only too glad to either *lead* or *assist* whenever the Lord shall further reveal His will concerning this consecrated spot of ground.[14]

At the April 1896 conference of the church the following comment was noted in the record:

> A strong sentiment was developed among the Church members towards fitting and preparing themselves for the mighty events that are so fast nearing our doors, and which will have for their central point of action, the Temple Lot and the building of the temple.[15]

Shortly after the final court decision and the first newspaper publication of the Church of Christ, Elder S. G. Spencer[16] of the LDS Church traveled to Independence, Missouri, to interview Joseph Smith III. The interview took place at the home of RLDS

---

[12] Jackson County, Property Records, 50:331-32; 53:526-27; 104:311, 517; 48:343 (this quit-claim deed covered the 3 lots purchased by John H. Hedrick); 115:452-54 (this quit-claim deed covered the 5 lots purchased by William Eaton), Independence, Missouri; "A Mormon Temple for Missouri," *Kansas City Times*, November 17, 1877, 2.

[13] The *Searchlight*, as has been previously mentioned, was published by the Church of Christ at Independence, Missouri, beginning with the February 1896 issue. Monthly publication continued through March 1900.

[14] John R. Haldeman, "By Way of Explanation," *Searchlight* 1, no. 1 (February 1896): 1. Italics in original.

[15] John R. Haldeman, "Conference Notes," *Searchlight* 1, no. 4 (May 1896): 27.

[16] Although American men in the nineteenth and early twentieth centuries typically used only initials, I have used full names wherever possible for the reader's ease in differentiating these historical personages, often little known at present.

Church Apostle Joseph Luff. One of the questions asked by Spencer was: "Do you believe that you will assist us in building this Temple in Independence?" Smith replied:

> As to the question of who will build or assist to build the Temple here (at Independence), I have no opinion to express. I am quite willing that the people indicated by God as His people shall build it. If I and my brethren with me shall be thought worthy of building, or even assisting to build it, all right; I shall be satisfied for the will of God to prevail in the matter.[17]

---

[17] Heman C. Smith, *True Succession in Church Presidency of the Church of Jesus Christ of Latter Day Saints*, (Lamoni, Iowa: Board of Publication of the Reorganized Church of Jesus Christ of Latter Day Saints, 1912), 103-113, (primary quote 107) (Smith cites *Herald*, September 14, 1898); James E. Yates, "An Interview," *Torch of Truth* 4, no.5 (June 1929): 55-56. All excerpts quoted by the *Torch of Truth* are from Smith, *True Succession in Church Presidency of the Church of Jesus Christ of Latter Day Saints*. An additional quote has Apostle Luff interjecting: "Had you not better ask whether you will assist us? We claim to be the true Church in succession." Note: Information regarding the *Torch of Truth* is provided hereafter.

A Trip to Salt Lake City and a Meeting with LDS Church First Presidency

I N JANUARY 1900, a joint meeting was held in Lamoni, Iowa, between representatives of the Church of Christ, namely George P. Frisbey and John R. Haldeman, and the First Presidency of the RLDS Church. The call for the meeting came from the Church of Christ. It is recorded that they (the elders of the Church of Christ) "had been moved upon [by the Spirit]" to see what could be done to "unite in an effort to prosecute the work of gathering, and the building of the temple at Independence, Missouri."[1]

At this meeting delegates from the Church of Christ proposed that two of their number travel to Utah and meet with the First Presidency of the LDS Church. Their stated objective was to obtain from the leadership of the LDS Church a commitment to participate in a proposed historic meeting to be held in Independence, Missouri. George P. Frisbey[2] and George D.

---

[1] *History of the RLDS Church*, 5:488-89. The meeting was held on January 18 and 19, 1900. First Presidency of the RLDS Church: Joseph Smith III, President, Alexander H. Smith, First Counselor, and Edmund L. Kelley, Second Counselor.

[2] George P. Frisbey was born in Marrietta, Ohio, in 1834 and was baptized a member of the Church of Christ in Tazewell County, Illinois, in 1865 by David Judy. Frisbey left Illinois in company with other members of the Church of Christ and traveled to Independence, Missouri, in 1867. He was a successful merchant in Independence, Missouri. A few years prior to his death in 1919, Frisbey served as the presiding elder of the Church of Christ.

James A. Hedrick, George D. Cole, and George P. Frisbey, BILL CURTIS

Cole[3] undertook this trip as representatives of the Church of Christ and not as representatives of the joint meeting.[4]

In the afternoon of February 8, 1900, Elder George D. Cole and Elder George P. Frisbey, having arrived by train from Independence, called on the First Presidency of the LDS Church and met in the office of President Lorenzo Snow, as previously arranged. They were accompanied by Charles W. Penrose who may have arranged the meeting and time. While pleasantries were undoubtedly exchanged, the purpose of the meeting was soon made known. The secretary who recorded the minutes of this meeting stated that Frisbey and Cole "had come from

[3] George D. Cole was a long-time member of the Church of Christ. He was baptized in April 1870, in Independence, Missouri, by Richard Hill. Cole was a very successful missionary and traveled extensively for the Church of Christ. He died in 1918.

[4] *Journal History*, Church of Jesus Christ of Latter-day Saints (chronological scrapbook of typed entries and newspaper clippings, 1830-present), February 8, 1900, 2; February 9, 1900, 1 (this meeting was cancelled); February 10, 1-6; February 21, 2-24, Church History Library, Salt Lake City, Utah (hereafter cited as *Journal History*). A secretary or stenographer (unnamed) was present at all of these meetings. First Presidency minutes, usually not available to researchers, were included in the *Journal History* for only a brief period.

View of the Temple Lot to the north-northwest, September 1, 1893, Bill Curtis

Independence, Missouri, for the purpose of ascertaining if it is not possible for a delegation of our [LDS] Church, a delegation of the 'Reorganite' church and a delegation of their own organization could not meet together for the purpose of trying to harmonize their views on doctrine with a view of coming together and uniting into one body.[5]

In discussing their objectives more specifically they admitted that "they were but custodians of the Temple ground in Independence" and that "the Spirit seemed to manifest to them…that they ought to take some steps towards placing this ground [the Temple Lot] so it can be used for the purpose indicated in the revelations." This meeting lasted "fully an hour during which time these men manifested a very good spirit." At the conclusion of this introductory gathering, President Snow appointed a meeting for the following day "at which President Cannon and whoever of the Apostles in reach may be present."[6]

[5] Ibid., February 8, 1900, 2.

[6] Ibid., February 8, 1900, 2. First Presidency of the LDS Church: Lorenzo Snow, President; George Q. Cannon, First Counselor; and Joseph F. Smith, Second

View of the Temple Lot to the east, ca 1902-1907, Photograph by C. Ed Miller showing 1902 Church of Christ meetinghouse, BILL CURTIS

This meeting was postponed until the 10th due to the absence of George Q. Cannon.

On the morning of February 10 all three members of the LDS Church First Presidency, plus Bishop William B. Preston of the Presiding Bishopric, met with Elders Frisbey and Cole. President Snow asked Frisbey and Cole "to state the object of their coming here for the benefit of all who were present." Cole responded that:

> They thought they had been moved upon by the proper spirit to come to Utah to see what, if anything, can be done about building the Temple at Jackson county, MO…that they were the guardians of the Temple Lot in Independence, and as such they felt that they could say that the Lord had instructed them to come and invite a delegation from Utah to meet with a delegation from their church and delegation from the Reorganites, at Independence for the purpose of trying to come to some understanding as to what ought to be done.[7]

Counselor. It is unclear from the notes whether George Q. Cannon was present for this initial meeting.

[7] Ibid., February 10, 1900, 1-6.

Considerable exchange followed between those in attendance. Questions were asked and answers freely given. At length, Frisbey commented that the "Temple would be built there in Independence, and that they [the Church of Christ] believed that money could not induce them to part with the land [the 2½ acre Temple Lot] although they had received offers even as high at one time as high as $100,000." Shortly thereafter, President Snow remarked "that he was of the opinion that the time was fast approaching…when the Lord would require the building of the Temple at Jackson county."[8] In answering President Snow's concern about agreement with the RLDS Church on the matter of organization, Frisbey replied that:

> The Lord might enable them to work together for the carrying out of this purpose, that is, the building of the Temple; and if the Temple could be build [sic], his idea was that the Savior would come to the Temple and He would set all things in order.[9]

By February 21st the much anticipated third meeting was held at 10:30 a.m. Those in attendance included the three members of the First Presidency; Apostles Francis M. Lyman, John Henry Smith, George Teasdale, Marriner W. Merrill, John W. Taylor, Anthon H. Lund, Abraham O. Woodruff of the Quorum of the Twelve; and William B. Preston and John R. Winder of the Presiding Bishopric. President Snow briefly outlined the meeting's purpose and again asked Elders Frisbey and Cole to express their feelings. LDS Church officials asked many questions of their visitors. At the meeting's conclusion, the First Presidency asked the Church of Christ representatives to allow them to discuss the proposal privately, and then meet again the next day. However, after checking individual calendars, Snow reassembled the church officials at 2:15 p.m. that afternoon.

---

[8] Ibid., February 10, 1900, 1-6.

[9] Ibid., February 10, 1900, 1-6.

View of the Temple Lot to the east, ca. 1904. RLDS Stone Church (on left) and Church of Christ chapel in the trees (center), Community of Christ Library-Archives

After a thorough and frank discussion, Snow reached a decision that was sustained by those present.[10]

At 4:30 p.m. "Elders Frisby [sic] and Cole of the Hedrickite church returned to the office, having been called for." President Snow "conversed privately with them and advised them that their proposal would not be accepted." Snow then "expressed the desire for the Church to pay their expenses here and back to their home," which were estimated to be $88.00.[11] The offer was graciously accepted and acknowledged at the joint committee follow-up meeting.[12]

The representatives returned to Independence soon thereafter, disappointed but not surprised. The first of the

---

[10] Ibid., February 21, 2–24.

[11] Ibid., February 21, 23-4.

[12] Minutes of Joint Council Meeting of the Church of Christ and Reorganized Church, March 6 – May 4, 1900, holograph, unnumbered pages (hereafter cited as Minutes of 1900), Miscellany Collection, P19, f54, Community of Christ Library-Archives, Independence, Missouri. Note: There are two independent sets of minutes. The minutes use "joint committee" and "joint council" interchangeably. Printed references which discuss these meetings also use the terms interchangeably. See also *History of the RLDS Church*, 5:489.

joint council meetings between the six chosen representatives of the RLDS Church and the six chosen representatives of the Church of Christ commenced in Independence on March 6, 1900.[13] The emissaries to Utah (Frisbey and Cole) reported their lack of success in obtaining any commitment from the LDS Church leadership to participate in the proposed "three church" meeting.[14] This "lack of success" did not come as a surprise to either group of representatives. One of the Church of Christ elders remarked: "that results were be about as [we had] expected" and that "L. D. [sic] Snow stood in the way."[15]

The necessity of building the temple, a constant theme reiterated at the Salt Lake City sessions, however, was clearly on the minds of those in attendance at the March 6 joint council gathering as stated in the minutes, namely: "[This] meeting [has been] called expressly in the interests of building [the] temple. Our object is to see if we can unite on plans to build the temple." Furthermore, "neither are we to expect a perfect understanding of the ministry on the theory, principle, and doctrine of the church, until the Temple is built, for it is there, in that house, that God has promised to perfect ALL who are called to the work of the ministry, in theory, principle, and doctrine," and "that the building of the Temple at Independence, Missouri, should be accomplished by the people of God." (RLDS D&C 94:3a-b and LDS D&C 97:10-12).[16]

The trip to Salt Lake City was apparently not made on a confidential basis. On March 1, 1900, the *Independence Sentinel*

---

[13] Minutes of 1900. At the January meeting in Lamoni, it was agreed that if the LDS Church should choose to participate in the proposed assembly in Independence, each of the three churches would send four representatives. If the LDS Church chose not to attend then the Church of Christ and the RLDS Church would each send six representatives. In either case the number of participants at the proposed historic gathering would be the symbolic "twelve."

[14] *History of the RLDS Church*, 5:489.

[15] Ibid. Lorenzo Snow had no middle initial, but the tone of the minutes suggests only a slip of the mind.

[16] Ibid. Capital letters in the original.

View of the Temple Lot to the north-northwest, 1904, by Underwood and Underwood publishers, BILL CURTIS

carried the headline: "Probable Amalgamation: Mormon Factions in Conference at Salt Lake City."[17] While the article indicated, in error, that representatives of the RLDS Church were also in attendance, the most interesting comment reported was that "if the present plan of amalgamation is successful this site [the Temple Lot] will be turned over to the Utah church and a fine temple [will be] erected there preparatory to the final gathering of all the saints of the earth at that point."[18] Approximately two weeks later Joseph Smith III visited Independence and was interviewed by the local *Independence Sentinel.* He flatly denied any involvement in the Salt Lake City meeting and discounted any possibility of an amalgamation.[19]

[17] "Probable Amalgamation," *Independence Sentinel (Independence, Missouri),* March 1, 1900, 2.

[18] Ibid.

[19] "Denies Rumor of Union: Joseph Smith [III] Says Latter Day Saints Will Not Join the Mormons," *Independence Sentinel,* March 16, 1900, 6.

1900–1916 Statements Regarding the Temple

DURING THE NEXT seventeen years comments regarding the importance and necessity of building the temple on that sacred space known as the Temple Lot continued to be expressed in the press, in minutes of conferences, and in letters written by leaders of the Church of Christ and the RLDS Church. In a June 1904 article titled: "Redemption of Zion," after castigating both the RLDS and LDS Churches, the editor stated:

> The Church of Christ, as custodians of the spot upon which the temple is to stand, realize the important position occupied, and have endeavored to arouse such interest in the building of the temple, as will result in at least preliminary steps being taken toward its erection.[1]

In March 1905, in another *Evening and Morning Star* article headed: "Importance of the Temple," the editor raised the question: "Is it possible that the individuals who are so busily engaged in their efforts in the behalf of Zion realize how important a factor is the building of the Temple?"[2] The editor (John R. Haldeman) then discussed five points concerning the Lord's demands regarding the building of the temple and then concluded with this statement: "how can so-called Latter Day Saints permit the months and years to pass without making some

---

[1] John R. Haldeman, "Redemption of Zion," *Evening and Morning Star* 5, no. 2 (June 20, 1904): 2.

[2] John R. Haldeman, "Importance of the Temple," *Evening and Morning Star* 5, no. 11 (March 1905): 3.

Temple Lot property featuring Church of Christ meeting-House, April 26, 1907, Photo by George Edward Anderson, LDS CHURCH HISTORY LIBRARY

movement towards building the house unto the Lord which is for the 'Salvation of Zion.'"[3] This theme continued throughout the year.

In the December 1905 issue of the *Evening and Morning Star*, Haldeman reiterated the sacred responsibility of the Church of Christ as "a trust which increases in magnitude, as year after year glides on and brings closer and closer that great event which all Latter Day Saints look forward to with joyful anticipation—the building of the Temple."[4] He added: "As the situation exists today, the Church of Christ stands in a position to attempt the building of the Temple, or, if it chooses, to pass that great work into the hands of either one of the great factions, the Utah church, or the Reorganization!"

By 1907 the building of the temple had been linked to living the Law of Consecration as given previously by revelation to Joseph Smith Jr. In the July number of the *Evening and Morning Star* an article appeared dealing with the means by which the temple would be finally built. The editor remarked: "We think

[3] Ibid.

[4] John R. Haldeman, (No Title), *Evening and Morning Star* 6, no. 8 (December 1905): 1.

John R. Haldeman

the question of raising the means to build the house is among the first problems to be solved. How shall it be done? The Church of Christ knows of but one method to raise the money, [sic] and that method is contained in the Book of Doctrine and Covenants." He continued: "The Consecration Law was the method proposed and required by the Almighty as the means to raise funds for that purpose…The Church of Christ believes the original provision is still in force"[5]

Later in September 1907 the editor, in again discussing the temple and the "One Mighty and Strong," interjected the matter of the "time frame" in which the temple should be built. Concluding that the definition of a "generation," as used in the Smith revelations was "100 years," he stated that: "when the Temple is built (and it must be built within the next 25 years to fulfill prophecy)."[6] The concern over the "generation" definition continued to be a subject of considerable discussion for years to come.

The year 1910 brought a different approach to the "urgency issue" regarding the temple. By this time, the leaders of both

[5] John R. Haldeman, "An Important Report," *Evening and Morning Star* 8, no. 3 (July 1907): 2.

[6] John R. Haldeman, "Concerning Apostles," *Evening and Morning Star* 8, no. 5 (September 1907): 2.

the Church of Christ and the RLDS Church were both well-advanced in age. On May 22, 1910, Joseph Smith III penned a letter to Richard E. Hill (presiding elder of the Church of Christ).[7] In this letter he called attention to the great need to build the temple. He said:

> The time is rapidly passing away in which according to legendary and tradition of teaching, a Temple was to be erected, as it has been supposed, on the spot known as the Temple Lot.

Smith continued:

> It would seem that there is small prospect of such Temple being erected by either the body you represent, or the body I represent. The one for want of means, the other for want of opportunity. The question arises, may there not be some common ground of agreement upon which both these bodies may stand to work together for the accomplishment of the one end? Can that common ground be reached in time for the accomplishment of the end desired? What say you?[8]

Hill responded two days later:

> What you have to say regarding the rapidly approaching date for the building of the Temple at Independence, Mo., is of interest to me. As to who will build that sacred edifice, naturally my hopes and desires are in behalf of my brethren of the Church of Christ, that there might be a common ground, after certain concessions were made as suggested by you, upon which men from both organizations might stand and work together for the accomplishment of that end.[9]

---

[7] Joseph Smith III, Letter to Richard E. Hill, May 22, 1910, Church of Christ Correspondence, 1910, Orders and Quorum Papers, P75-4, f26, Community of Christ Library-Archives, Independence, Missouri.

[8] Ibid.

[9] Richard E. Hill, Letter to Joseph Smith III, May 24, 1910, Church of Christ Correspondence, 1910, Orders and Quorum Papers, P75-4, f26, Community of Christ Library-Archives, Independence, Missouri.

The RLDS First Presidency in 1909: Elbert A. Smith, Joseph Smith III, Frederick M. Smith, COMMUNITY OF CHRIST LIBRARY-ARCHIVES

Nothing further is known regarding this effort. Hill died a few months later in February 1911. Smith passed away in December 1914.[10]

Various aspects of the necessity of building the temple continued to occupy meetings and publications between 1914 and the closing months of 1917. In 1914, for example, the issue of "generation" was discussed in regards to the remaining time frame in which to erect the temple as stated in scripture.[11] The minutes of a Church of Christ meeting for March 7, 1915, contained language dealing with the linkage between the Law of Consecration and the building of the temple. A motion was voted upon and approved by the body which stated:

---

[10] Richard E. Hill died February 11, 1911. See "Elder Richard Hill," *Evening and Morning Star* 11, no. 10 (February 1911): 1. Joseph Smith III died December 10, 1914. See *History of the RLDS Church*, 6:577.

[11] "Temple to be Built in This Generation," *Evening and Morning Star* 16, no. 3 (June 1914): 1.

Where as [sic] we believe the Law of Consecration was given for the purpose of bringing equality in the Church of Christ and is essential to be carried out before the Temple can be built for Christ's coming; Be it there fore [sic] resolved, that we accept it as binding upon us and make the necessary preparations to put it into effect...that we may become equal in earthly possessions in order that we may have an equal opportunity in obtaining Heavenly things, and to further on the work of Zion's Redemption.[12]

In 1916, the *Evening and Morning Star* again published the 1870 George D. Cole dream regarding his vision of the temple.[13]

---

[12] Minutes, Church of Christ, Independence, Missouri, March 7, 1915. Photocopy of typed transcription in possession of author.

[13] George D. Cole, "Times of the Gentiles be Fulfilled," *Evening and Morning Star* 17, no. 12 (March 1916): 5-6.

1918 Agreements of Working Harmony and Their Impact on Building the House of the Lord

BY LATE 1917 a new era of possibilities and cooperation between the two churches had developed once more. At the April 1917 conference of the RLDS Church, the "Committee on the Church of Christ was reconstituted."[1] This decision was followed with tangible action. During the summer of 1917, the Church of Christ and the RLDS Church jointly sponsored tent or union meetings. These meetings were held on the Temple Lot.[2] A renewed feeling of better understanding and increased fellowship developed between the members of both churches and a revived interest in building the temple occurred during this period of rapprochement.[3] Unfortunately, the meetings were canceled in September as a result of dissatisfaction by some members of the Church of Christ.[4] They suggested that the only reason the RLDS Church had participated was to gain possession of the Temple Lot.[5]

Regardless of the disappointing end to these union meetings, official representatives of both organizations were selected

---

[1] *History of the RLDS Church,* 7:192.

[2] Flint, *An Outline History of the Church of Christ,* 134.

[3] Minutes, Large Record, Church of Christ, 241 (cited by Flint, *An Outline History of the Church of Christ,* 134). See also *History of the RLDS Church,* 7:204.

[4] Ibid.

[5] Ibid.

*The RLDS First Presidency: Elbert A. Smith, Fred M. Smith, and Floyd M.
McDowell,* COMMUNITY OF CHRIST LIBRARY-ARCHIVES

sometime later that fall to meet in another effort toward
reconciliation. Their first meeting was held on December 30,
1917.⁶ These meetings continued through January 27, 1918,
and at their conclusion, a significant document was produced.
In the history of the Restoration, nothing like this "joint effort"
of two churches of the Restoration to produce a document
of agreement on doctrine and accommodation had ever been
undertaken, much less successfully accomplished, even if not
completely. In the official minutes the document was titled:
"Agreements of Working Harmony."⁷

---

⁶ *History of the RLDS Church*, 6:280.

⁷ Ibid. "Agreement<u>s</u>" in the plural is correct. The document is also referred to as
"Articles of Working Harmony" or "Agreements of 1918" in later reporting of this
event and is specifically referred to by that title in the *History of the RLDS Church*
7:280-282. Furthermore, the Church of Christ generally referred to that historic
document as the "Agreement of Working Harmony" (no plural "s") or, more often,
simply "Working Agreement." For consistency, the author has attempted to use the
name as shown in the official minutes, i.e., "Agreements of Working Harmony." See
Flint, *An Outline History of the Church of Christ*, 119-121, 134; the Stebbins papers,
P24, f34, Community of Christ Library-Archives, Independence, Missouri.

View of the Temple site to the north-northeast, ca 1910. SPECIAL COLLECTIONS AND ARCHIVES, MERRILL CAZIER LIBRARY, UTAH STATE UNIVERSITY

At the April conferences of both churches, these "Agreements of Working Harmony" were presented and adopted.[8] An announcement in the *Independence Examiner* dated April 9, 1918, carried a sub-headline: "Hedrickite and Reorganized in Agreement."[9] While the Church of Christ legally maintained control of the Temple Lot, monumental changes in the relationships of the two bodies occurred. The document provided for the transfer of membership between the two churches with no requirement for rebaptism, since "each recognize the standing of the other" (item 9 in the "Agreements").[10] This specific item was to have major and critical implications in the years ahead.

[8] *General Conference Minutes*, April 6, 1918, Reorganized Church of Jesus Christ of Latter Day Saints, Independence, Missouri, 2607-2611; and General Church Record, March 31, 1918, Church of Christ on the Temple Lot, Independence, Missouri, 257-266; Flint, *An Outline History of the Church of Christ*, 119-121.

[9] "Next Conference, Iowa: Building of an Assembly Hall Being Considered — Hedrickite and Reorganized in Agreement," *Independence Examiner* (Independence, Missouri), April 9, 1918.

[10] *History of the RLDS Church*, 7:280-282; Flint, *An Outline History of the Church of Christ*, 119-120.

Church of Christ Presiding Elder Clarence L. Wheaton,
CHURCH OF CHRIST (TEMPLE LOT)

View of the Temple Lot to the northeast, ca early 1900s. Caretaker and tool sheds in foreground, RLDS Stone Church on left, BILL CURTIS

From a more administrative and secular perspective, the two groups began exchanging preachers at their respective Sunday services.[11] Also, as noted by Samuel A. Burgess, RLDS Church historian, in a letter written on August 29, 1925, to RLDS Church Bishop Charles J. Hunt of Michigan, he discussed certain aspects of the "Agreements." Burgess stated that the "Agreements of 1918" provided for the joint use of facilities including buildings and baptismal fonts.[12] In fact, according to Burgess, the RLDS Church "has paid what taxes have been assessed and kept up the fence where there was a fence. I note our janitors cutting the lawn."[13]

During the first few years of this period of "working harmony" and the mutual "good feelings" manifested by both churches, Church of Christ Presiding Elder Clarence L. Wheaton received

---

[11] Samuel A. Burgess, Letter to Robert Orme, December 30, 1924, Miscellaneous Samuel A. Burgess Collection, P104, Community of Christ Library-Archives, Independence, Missouri.

[12] Samuel A. Burgess, Letter to Bishop Charles J. Hunt, August 29, 1925, Miscellaneous Samuel A. Burgess Collection, P104, Community of Christ Library-Archives, Independence, Missouri.

[13] Ibid.

a revelation (March 1919) dealing specifically with the temple. He was told to:

> Lay aside all contention with your brethren of the different branches of my church, for in the day that I shall come to my temple I will perfect them in theory and in doctrine.

Furthermore, he was told that:

> Ye shall be the means of saving your brethren, and bringing them to a unity of purpose and action before me, for the time of building the temple and the fulfilling of the prophets is at hand and the work must be accomplished speedily.[14]

While nothing in particular developed from this revelation, it certainly made apparent, to both the Church of Christ and the RLDS Church, that the Lord's intention was to keep the building of the temple foremost in their collective thinking. With the thought of "coming together" to build the temple, Church of Christ member E. Stafford wrote a letter to Clyde Ellis, then serving a mission for the RLDS Church in Tahiti. After discussing his baptism into the Church of Christ and relating events of the past few years occasioned by the "Agreements of Working Harmony," he added that: "some day we will all come together and build the Temple."[15]

---

[14] Clarence L. Wheaton, "The Mission of the Church of Christ," *Zion's Advocate* 2, no. 8 (September 15, 1925): 12; "The Mission of the Church of Christ," sermon delivered by Apostle Clarence L. Wheaton (Sunday morning, July 19, 1925): 7. This is a personal typewritten manuscript. Photocopy in possession of the author.

15 E. Stafford, Letter to Clyde Ellis, March 9, 1922, Clyde F. Ellis Papers, P38, f12, items 8-13, Community of Christ Library-Archives, Independence, Missouri.

Supreme Directional Control and the Cancellation of the Agreements of Working Harmony

T HE PERIOD OF near unity between the two churches ended, however, as a direct result of an administrative position adopted by President Fredrick M. Smith[1] of the RLDS Church regarding control over all church matters. By at least 1924, this view came to be called Supreme Directional Control (or SDC).[2] In simple terms, President Frederick M. Smith took a stricter approach, than did his father Joseph Smith III, regarding the decision making process in directing the church.

This approach did not "sit well" with some of the members of the RLDS Church. Certain individuals, particularly the Presiding Bishopric of the RLDS Church, strongly resisted "SDC."[3]

---

[1] Frederick M. Smith was born January 21, 1874, at Plano, Illinois, the son of Joseph Smith III and Bertha Madison Smith. He was the grandson of Joseph and Emma Hale Smith. Smith received his B.A. from Graceland College (the RLDS Church college in Lamoni, Iowa — he was the college's first graduate). In 1902 he was made a counselor in the First Presidency to his father Joseph Smith III, president of the RLDS Church. In 1911 Smith obtained his M.A. from the University of Kansas and in 1916 his Ph.D. from Clark University. After the death of his father, he was ordained Prophet/President of the RLDS Church on May 5, 1915. Smith died on March 20, 1946.

[2] *History of the RLDS Church*, 7:600, 625-638.

[3] Ibid., vol. 7, 651-655; "Chip Falls at Church Session: Fight Begins with Seating of Smith as Chairman," *Kansas City Post (Kansas City, Missouri)*, April 6, 1925, stated: "Benjamin R. McGuire, presiding bishop of the church is leading opponent of the document." The "Document on Church Government" was scheduled for presentation at the conference session the following day by President Frederick M. Smith.

Many others within the membership of the church likewise disagreed. With the "door open" to transferring membership to the Church of Christ, as provided for in the "Agreements of Working Harmony," many dissatisfied and disaffected members simply "moved across the street." Almost overnight the official Church of Christ membership soared.[4] Many who "came over" were prominent in the RLDS Church which caused great consternation to President Smith, his councilors and others in the leadership of the church.[5]

With the influx of many seasoned members from the RLDS Church, administrative changes soon took place within the Church of Christ. At the October 1925 semiannual conference of the Church of Christ, "a resolution was adopted abolishing the office of Presiding Elder."[6] Later that same day (October 8), another resolution was introduced (and voted upon in the affirmative) "to perfect the organization in harmony with the teachings of the Bible and Book of Mormon."[7] A secondary consideration was the explosive growth of the Church of Christ. In the period from 1916 to 1925 the church had grown from about 100 members to perhaps 500 members.[8] The growth, as

---

[4] Flint, *An Outline History of the Church of Christ*, 138-9.

[5] Ibid.

[6] "Minutes of a Special Conference of the Church of Christ at Independence, Missouri, Beginning Tuesday, October 6th, 1925," *Zion's Advocate* 2, no. 10 (November 15, 1925): 9.

[7] "Minutes of a Special Conference of the Church of Christ at Independence, Missouri, Beginning Tuesday, October 6th, 1925," *Zion's Advocate* 2, no. 10 (November 15, 1925): 9. Flint, *An Outline History of the Church of Christ*, 139.

[8] "Plans Are from God Three Churchmen Say," *Independence Examiner*, April 3, 1929; "Temple by Revelation," *Independence Examiner*, April 10, 1928, 1; Clarence L. Wheaton, "Delegates or Referendum," *Zion's Advocate* 6, no. 9 (September 1929): 129. Note: In the "Plans Are from God Three Churchmen Say," *Independence Examiner* article of April 3, 1929, Apostle Clarence L. Wheaton stated: "Three years ago we had only one hundred members. We now have one thousand." The official membership totals for 1928 and 1929 were 889 and 1232 respectively. Wheaton's estimate of 100 "three years ago" (1926) was incorrect. Allowing for continual growth (transferees from the RLDS Church) after the 1925/1926 period, the above estimate of 500 members by the year 1925 seems more reasonable. Bert C. Flint, *An*

previously noted, was primarily the result of the transferees from the RLDS Church.

The resolution stated: "that we petition the Lord for direction as to the choosing of the Apostles."[9] After a thirty minute "season of prayer," and toward the close of that day's business, the following revelation was received by Elder Daniel Macgregor,[10] a recent transferee from the RLDS Church:

> Verily thus saith the Spirit, in order that the Church of Christ may be prepared to more effectively occupy, it is the wish of the Spirit that my servants H[iram] E. Moler, and F[rank] F. Wipper, shall be a committee to select a Committee of Three, who shall serve as Apostles before me.[11]

It was thereafter moved that the church "accept the communication given through Elder Daniel Macgregor...as instructions coming from the Lord to us."[12] The motion was then referred to the "eldership in a special session." Two days later a report of the "Elder's Council" was read and a vote taken. The vote tally was: "38½ for and none against."[13]

Outline History of the Church of Christ, 139, stated: "During this period the Church of Christ grew rapidly, and from a membership of a couple of hundred in 1915, by 1926 it had grown to several thousand, and continued to grow." Based on the above-cited information, Flint's estimates are significantly exaggerated.

[9] "Minutes of a Special Conference of the Church of Christ at Independence, Missouri, Beginning Tuesday, October 6th, 1925," *Zion's Advocate* 2, no. 10 (November 15, 1925): 9; Flint, *An Outline History of the Church of Christ*, 139.

[10] Daniel Macgregor joined the RLDS Church as a 16-year-old in 1891. He was ordained a seventy in 1898 and was well known as a great missionary, orator, and author. He left the RLDS Church in 1925 during the "SDC controversy" and became one of the apostles chosen by the Church of Christ in 1926. Macgregor died unexpectedly in 1927.

[11] Flint, *An Outline History of the Church of Christ*, 139. Flint cites "Record No. 5," Church of Christ, 89.

[12] "Minutes of a Special Conference of the Church of Christ at Independence, Missouri, Beginning Tuesday, October 6th, 1925," *Zion's Advocate* 2, no. 10 (November 15, 1925): 9.

[13] Ibid., 11.

Church of Christ (Temple Lot) General Conference, April 6, 1927

At the April 1926 conference, the Church of Christ organized a Council or Quorum of Twelve Apostles.[14] Initially seven men were ordained. Six of the seven new apostles were transferees from the RLDS Church. One of the six was Otto Fetting. He

---

[14] Flint, *An Outline History of the Church of Christ*, 140. The office of "apostle" had not been utilized by the Church of Christ for approximately 50 years. Like the RLDS Church, in the early years of the Church of Christ, the office of apostle was the primary priesthood office. The RLDS Church or "New Organization" implemented its Quorum of Apostles in 1853 with the calling of 7 men to that office. Eventually the quorum was expanded to 12 men and the quorum was maintained thereafter, both in its number, i.e., 12, and responsibility (*History of the RLDS Church*, 3:218.). That organization, i.e., the Quorum of the Twelve Apostles, continues to exist today in the Community of Christ.

Historically, the Church of Christ initially chose 5 men as apostles, including John E. Page, Granville Hedrick, David Judy, Adna C. Haldeman, and Jedediah Owen (*Crow Creek Record*, 14). The Church of Christ ordained one other individual (Walter McDaniels) to the priesthood office of apostle in 1869. ("Minutes of the Church of Christ," November 1869). After that date no other individuals were so ordained and the office of apostle was dropped in favor of the office of "presiding elder."

Church of Christ (Temple Lot) General Conference, April 6, 1927, BILL CURTIS

was soon to play a critical, controversial, and pivotal role in the future of the Church of Christ.[15]

The re-introduction of the priesthood office of "apostle" by the Church of Christ brought their amicable relationship with the RLDS Church to an abrupt end. As long as there was only one Quorum of Apostles in the church (from the RLDS Church perspective), the leadership of the RLDS Church felt they could deal with the issue of membership transfer. Based on the "Agreements of Working Harmony" the Church of Christ was considered a branch of the church.[16] In the eyes of the RLDS Church, the choosing of a nucleus of a Quorum of

---

[15] The seven men were: Daniel Macgregor, Hiram E. Moler, Samuel Wood, Frank F. Wipper, Norris Headding, Otto Fetting (all transferees from the RLDS Church) and Clarence L. Wheaton (the only individual from the Church of Christ). Prior to and during the period of the Agreements of Working Harmony of 1918, Wheaton had served as the presiding elder of the Church of Christ (from 1915–1925.)

[16] Of the original 24 points in the "Agreements of Working Harmony" this is item number 22.

Twelve Apostles made reconciliation between the two churches more difficult, if not impossible: "Having set up a general church organization, the Church of Christ could no longer be regarded as an unattached but related group of the Restoration movement."[17]

This action by the Church of Christ, i.e., the choosing of apostles (in the opinion of the RLDS Church officials), together with the abrogation of article 4 (which referred to the acceptance of the 1835 edition of the Doctrine and Covenants vs. the 1833 edition of the Book of Commandments) of the Agreements of Working Harmony brought about a move to rescind the eight-year old agreement. By a vote of the delegates assembled, during the April 1926 RLDS Church conference, the Agreements of Working Harmony were "rescinded and declared null and void and no longer binding upon…the church."[18] Notwithstanding the termination of the Agreements of Working Harmony by the RLDS Church, transferees to the Church of Christ continued — and so did the rhetoric!

---

[17] *History of the RLDS Church*, vol. 8:77.

[18] Ibid., vol. 8:68. The "Agreements of Working Harmony" are referred to as the "Articles of Working Harmony" in the adopted resolution of the April 1926 conference of the RLDS Church.

Intensified Interest in Building the House of the Lord

DURING THE PERIOD 1925-1927 there developed within the Church of Christ, in particular, a more intensified interest in building the temple. In December 1925, the *Torch of Truth*, an independent newspaper edited and published by James E. Yates, a "protesting" RLDS Church member,[1] published a piece titled: "Place of the Temple."[2] In referring to the members of the Church of Christ in this article, he stated:

> They have held and protected the consecrated Lot, kept the faith, and are now ready, when the saints forsake the world's standards and rally to the Lord's work to proceed to build the temple in "this generation" instead of building a thousand and one other things. And they are waiting to help build the Temple in the exact place where the word of the Lord says it shall stand.[3]

---

[1] The *Torch of Truth (Independence, Missouri)* was edited and published by James E. Yates. Yates would transfer his membership to the Church of Christ in the late 1920s. He was ordained an apostle in the Church of Christ in April 1928. The *Torch of Truth*, although primarily published during its existence at Independence, Missouri, was relocated as Yates was assigned various mission fields. These locales included: San Bernardino, California; Los Angeles, California; Spokane, Washington; Potlatch, Idaho; and Phoenix, Arizona. See James E. Yates and Evalena Sills, *Cut from the Rough: The Life Story of James E. Yates* (Phoenix, Arizona: Big T Printers, 1984), 165-67.

[2] James E. Yates, "Place of the Temple," *Torch of Truth* 1, no. 8 (December 15, 1925): 4.

[3] Ibid.

View of the Temple Lot to the northeast, April 30, 1927. Grinter photograph,
BILL CURTIS

This feeling of "rallying" to soon build the temple carried over to the April 1926 conference of the Church. *Zion's Advocate,* in reporting on the success of the conference in its May 1926 issue reported: "The Church of Christ emerges from the general conference...with renewed hope born of the assurance that God's watchcare [sic] is overshadowing his work, and that his arm is extended to bring about the fulfillment of his promises that is [sic] to 'begin at the Temple Lot.'" (See RLDS D&C 83:2 and LDS D&C 84:3).[4]

In the October 1926 issue of the *Messenger,*[5] its editor and publisher Thomas W. Williams (formerly an apostle in the RLDS

---

[4] "The Conference of 1926," *Zion's Advocate* 3, no. 4 (May 1926): 1.

[5] The *Messenger* was edited and published in Independence, Missouri, by Thomas W. Williams, Vida E. Smith, and Edward D. Moore. The first issue was dated October 1925. It published continuously through January 1932. The *Messenger* was another monthly publication born out of the "Protest Movement" by dissatisfied members of the RLDS Church, i.e., those opposed to Supreme Directional Control ("SDC"). Thomas W. Williams had been a member of the Quorum of Twelve Apostles of the

Church), made this statement: "The members of the Church of Christ are inspired with the idea that a temple must be builded [sic] on a specific piece of ground and within the generation beginning with 1832 [1831] and honestly are bending their propaganda and effort with this in view."[6]

Two months later, in December 1926, another *Messenger* article dealing with temple building stated:

> The ministers and members of the Church of Christ are making some extravagant claims concerning the temple lot and the building of a temple.
>
> If there is to be a temple built within the generation commencing in 1832 [1831], then it is up to the Almighty to direct and[,] further[,] there must be more revealed than we have at the present time. And people are exceedingly foolish to center their claims on such a proposition without clear, explicit, and definite divine instruction.
>
> It would be well to dismiss this temple building until we know more about it.[7]

RLDS Church. The *Messenger* was much less sympathetic to the Church of Christ and especially to the former RLDS Church members who had transferred to the Church of Christ than was the *Torch of Truth*.

[6] Thomas W. Williams, "Builders of Temples Yesterday and Today," *Messenger* 2, no. 1 (*Independence, Missouri*) (October 1926): 7.

[7] Thomas W. Williams, "Twenty-four Temples Proposed for Zion," *Messenger* 2, no. 3 (December 1926): 47.

A Temple Will Soon Be Built

T O WHAT EXTENT the editorials of the *Messenger* and other publications played in the thinking of the members and the leadership of the Church of Christ is, of course, only speculative. Regardless, on the morning of February 4, 1927, at his home in Port Huron, Michigan, Church of Christ Apostle Otto Fetting launched the most dynamic movement toward building the temple on the Temple Lot since the dedication of that site by Joseph Smith Jr. in August 1831. Fetting reported an angelic visitation wherein he was told: "The revelation that was given for the building of the temple was true and the temple soon will be started."[1] (This reference was specifically in regard to the scripture in the Old Testament, Malachi 3:1.) This first meeting was followed by another visitation ("Message 2") the following month. In this vision, Fetting was shown the temple on the Temple Lot and people assembling to build it. He also saw the number "1929" written in the sky.[2]

In preparation for the 1927 conference of the church, the April issue of *Zion's Advocate* published the "Articles of Faith and Practice of the Church of Christ." There were twenty-five articles. Number 23 stated:

---

[1] "A Message from 'The Messenger,'" *Zion's Advocate* 4, no. 5 (May 1927): 69; *The Word of the Lord* (Independence, Missouri: Church of Christ With The Elijah Message, 1943, rpt. 1971), 7-8 (hereafter cited as *Word of the Lord*). The "First Message" was received at Otto Fetting's home in Port Huron, Michigan, on February 4, 1927. Fetting sequentially numbered all subsequent "Messages" as they were received.

[2] Otto Fetting, "A Message from 'The Messenger,'" *Zion's Advocate* 4, no. 5 (May 1927): 69-70; *Word of the Lord*, 8-10. The "Second Message" was received at Otto Fetting's home in Port Huron, Michigan, on March 4, 1927.

View of the Temple Lot to the northwest, ca 1927. Image shows construction underway on RLDS Auditorium, COMMUNITY OF CHRIST LIBRARY-ARCHIVES

We believe a temple will be built in this generation in Independence, Missouri, wherein Christ will reveal himself and endow his servants whom he chooses with power to preach the gospel in all the world to every kindred, tongue, and people, that the promises of God to Israel may be fulfilled.[3]

Following an announcement of the initial Fetting "Message" at the 1927 April conference, a recommendation of "the Twelve," pertaining to the temple, was presented to the conference. It read:

That a Temple fund shall be started at once and that those in charge of the finances be instructed to hold the subscriptions received in a trust fund. And that the funds so collected shall be reserved for the erection of the Temple of the Lord on the Temple Lot, and for no other purpose.[4]

---

[3] "Articles of Faith and Practice of the Church of Christ," *Zion's Advocate* 4, no. 4 (April 1927): 62-4, see article number 23. Previous publication of the "Articles of Faith and Practice of the Church of Christ" had appeared in the *Zion's Advocate* 2, no. 5 (June 15, 1925), 6.

[4] Clarence L. Wheaton, "Recommendations of the Twelve: April 9th, 1927," *Zion's Advocate* 4, no. 4 (April 1927): 68.

*1927 View of the Temple Lot to the south-southwest, showing the fenced
baptismal font of the Church of Christ,* CHURCH OF CHRIST (TEMPLE LOT)

The recommendation was moved and carried "to approve
the recommendation of the Twelve that a Temple Fund be
established."[5] Obviously, the leadership of the church was moving
forward in its hope that the time was near for the building of the
long-awaited House of the Lord.

In a most compelling article, dealing with the unparalleled
enthusiasm generated by the membership of the Church of
Christ regarding the Fetting "Messages" (a third "Message"
had been received in June), the *Messenger* in its October 1927
issue prophesied:

> They [the Church of Christ] have recently started a temple fund. It is
> perfectly psychological that the wish may be the father of the thought
> and before long one of their prophets will present a revelation to erect
> the building.[6]

[5] "Minutes of the General Conference of the Church of Christ [1927]," *Zion's
Advocate* 4, no. 5 (May 1927): 67-8; Otto Fetting, "Second Visit from the Same
Messenger on March 4, 1927," *Zion's Advocate* 4, no. 5 (May 1927): 70.

[6] Thomas W. Williams, "A Study in Temple Building," *Messenger* 3, no. 1 (October
1927): 6. In the May 1928 issue of the *Messenger* 4, no. 5, page 68, the editor

*Church of Christ Apostle Otto Fetting. Fetting received first "Message"
regarding the temple in 1927,* Paul Savage

Adding to the excitement of 1927 within the Church of Christ (and undoubtedly to the consternation of the RLDS Church), a rumor circulated throughout the several divisions of the Restoration that the Utah based LDS Church had offered $1 million dollars for the Temple Lot.[7] This rumor followed a period of concern and mistrust among some individuals within the leadership of the Church of Christ regarding a local Independence initiative to decentralize general church control and to enact congregational control on a "local" level.[8]

(Williams) makes particular note of his earlier prediction regarding the announcement by the Church of Christ on April 14, [10] 1928, that a "decision to build the temple was made as a result of a revelation by its quorum of twelve [Church of Christ] at its annual conference here." See also "Temple By Revelation: Church of Christ General Conference Receives What Is Considers [sic] a Divine Command to Build," *Independence Examiner*, April 10, 1928, 1.

[7] Thomas W. Williams, "A Study in Temple Building," *Messenger* 3, no. 1 (October 1, 1927): 5.

[8] F. L. Horton, "Affidavit: To Whom It May Concern," *Zion's Advocate* 4, no. 4 (April 1927): 53-54; Samuel Wood, "That Affidavit," *Zion's Advocate* 4, no. 4 (April 1927): 54-55. Congregations of the Church of Christ are called "locals" rather than "branches" or "wards."

Individuals in leadership positions within the Church of Christ (and the RLDS Church) speculated that former Apostle Frank F. Wipper, together with at least eight other members of the Independence congregation (all of whom had withdrawn from the church in the fall of 1926), were somehow involved in a scheme to acquire the Temple Lot and sell it to the highest bidder.[9] For over eighteen months speculation surrounded these rumors and innuendoes[10] and these concerns carried over to the 1927 and 1928 conferences of the church.[11]

It must be remembered that the "Temple and the Redemption of Zion"[12] were long-standing, traditional concepts of the RLDS Church (as well as all divisions of the Restoration). Therefore, for those previously devout members of the RLDS Church who had transferred their membership to the Church of Christ because of the dogma of "SDC," these doctrines were very familiar. The particular tenet of building "The Temple" was always in their collective thinking.[13] Most of these new members or transferees

---

[9] Samuel Wood, "Recapitulation: Meeting of the Quorum of Twelve," *Zion's Advocate* 4, no. 2 (February 1927): 19.

[10] Frank F. Wipper, et al., *Was the Temple Lot in Jeopardy?* (Independence, Missouri: Printed privately by Wipper, et al., 1927). *Was the Temple Lot in Jeopardy?* is an eight-page, legal-sized, typed document and was obviously intended for distribution. Harold B. Lee Library, L. Tom Perry Special Collections, AC 901. Ala no. 4383, Brigham Young University, Provo, Utah (hereafter cited as Special Collections, Brigham Young Library, Provo, Utah).

[11] "Editorial Briefs," *Zion's Advocate* 4, no. 5 (May 1927), 70; "Conference Nears End: A Troublesome Resolution Tabled This Morning," *Independence Examiner*, April 13, 1928, 1.

[12] Thomas W. Williams, "Editorials," *Messenger* 5, no. 6 (June 1929): 45. The eventual return to Jackson County, Missouri, and the erection of the House of the Lord on the Temple Lot in Independence, Missouri, had long been a motivating factor for the RLDS Church (and for all other divisions of the Restoration). As mentioned previously, Joseph Smith III had a dream/vision (1878) of what the temple was to look like and where it was to be located years before. The Temple Lot Case, also previously referred to, dealt specifically with the RLDS Church's avowal that they were the "legitimate" successor to the church Joseph Smith Jr. had founded in 1830 and, therefore, the rightful owners of the Temple Lot.

[13] Of those men chosen and ordained apostles by the Church of Christ in the period 1926-30, all but one of them was a transferee from the RLDS Church. The sole

of the Church of Christ now saw a realization of the early revelations to the Prophet Joseph Smith regarding the erection of the temple in Independence, Jackson County, Missouri, (and the promises thereof) which they had been unable, personally, to envision while they were members of the RLDS Church. And this was, of course, because the Church of Christ owned the Temple Lot.

However, it would be wrong to assume that the "Messenger's" command to "build the temple" by the Church of Christ had diminished, in any way, the mindset of RLDS Church President Frederick M. Smith regarding the vision of the RLDS Church and their eventual desire to build the temple at Independence. Prior to Fetting's receipt of the "First Message," President Smith, in his April 6, 1926, conference address to the church stated:

> And must I mention still before us the great task of building ultimately the Temple to which we have all looked forward? I have not forgotten it. I do not forget it. For in my dreams of Zion it is always in a prominent place of perceptive.
>
> Can words make it any plainer than the foregoing that the building of the Temple is yet in the future? We will await developments.[14]

---

member who was not a transferee was Clarence L. Wheaton, the former presiding elder of the Church of Christ.

Clarence L. Wheaton was born July 6, 1893, in Mound City, Missouri. His grandfather's brother was Adna C. Haldeman, an original member of the Church of Christ and one of the four men ordained to the apostleship by John E. Page in 1863. Wheaton was a printer by trade. Wheaton had been baptized a member of the Church of Christ in 1906 and was elected the presiding elder of the church at age 21 in 1915. He was ordained an apostle in 1926 and spent most of his life as an administrator and missionary for the Church of Christ. He died September 26, 1977.

[14] F. M. Ball, "Is This the Temple?," *Messenger* 4, no. 3 (March 1928): 40.

"Fifth Message" and the Command to Build the Temple Beginning in 1929

THE "DEVELOPMENTS" anticipated by President Frederick M. Smith were not the ones taking place across the street on the Temple Lot. That the excitement caused by Fetting's "Messages" (numbers 1 & 2 had been received prior to the 1927 conference and numbers 3 & 4 in the summer and fall of 1927)[1] had not ebbed was evidenced by a significant article which appeared on the front page of the March 1928 issue of *Zion's Advocate*. The headline presented to the subscribers was: "Building the Temple."[2] The author, Apostle Hiram E. Moler, began by posing this query: "But when shall it take place? That is the great question." The author noted that a "trust fund for the building of the Temple" had already been established and then speculated as to the "pattern for the Temple?" He then stated that "we have no one man whom we adore as God's exclusive mouthpiece." He concluded his article by speculating:

> We have sometimes wondered if the plan and specifications would all
> be given to one, or more, individuals, or whether the specifications for
> certain parts or portions would be given to various individuals, such
> as the size and space of the excavation to one or a group of persons,

[1] *Word of the Lord*, 10-13. The "Third Message" was received at Otto Fetting's home in Port Huron, Michigan, on June 12, 1927, and the "Fourth Message" was received at Otto Fetting's home in Port Huron, Michigan, on November 16, 1927.

[2] Hiram E. Moler, "Building the Temple," *Zion's Advocate* 5, no. 3 (March 1928): 33.

to others the foundation, and still to others the shell of the building, and so on until the whole work shall be accomplished. This would certainly eliminate all 'one-man direction,' and give equal opportunity to all.[3]

Notwithstanding Apostle Moler's thoughts and, perhaps, concerns, the "Messages" regarding the temple continued to be received by Apostle Fetting. On March 22, 1928, the historic "Fifth Message" was announced.[4] It had been previously revealed to Fetting in "Message Two," verse 2, that the church was commanded to erect "the temple" on the sacred space owned by the Church of Christ and known throughout the various divisions of the Restoration as, simply, the Temple Lot.[5]

Furthermore, the "Fifth Message" (verses 5 and 11), specifically proclaimed that construction on the temple was to begin in the year 1929 — confirming the "1929" written in the clouds in Fetting's vision that accompanied the "Second Message," (verse 7)[6] and that the church was given seven years to build the temple (verse 5).[7] That particular verse, which specifically set the seven-year completion deadline at 1936, continually prompted and pushed the leadership of the Church of Christ to renew their efforts to build "The Temple." The church's efforts were constantly directed (but not without occasional lapses) from March 22, 1928, through the year 1936 (and beyond) to build "The Temple." First, by calling upon the

---

[3] Ibid.

[4] Otto Fetting, "Manifestation Received By Apostle Otto Fetting," *Zion's Advocate* 5, no. 5 (May 1928): 69-70; *Word of the Lord*, 13-16. The "Fifth Message" was received at Fetting's home in Port Huron, Michigan, on March 22, 1928.

[5] *Word of the Lord*, 7-9.

[6] Otto Fetting, "Second Visit from the Same Messenger on March 4, 1927," *Zion's Advocate* 4, no. 5 (May 1927): 70; *Word of the Lord*, 9-10.

[7] Otto Fetting, "Manifestation Received By Apostle Otto Fetting," *Zion's Advocate* 5 (May 1928): 70; *Word of the Lord*, 14-15.

membership of their church and, second, all other churches of the Restoration.[8]

Fetting's "Fifth Message" electrified the membership of the Church of Christ like nothing had before. The revelation was read on April 9, 1928, to the church at the annual April conference and affirmatively voted upon as "divine."[9] From the moment this message was broadcast throughout the church, the physical undertaking to build the House of the Lord would play a major and pivotal role within the church; both among the members and more especially among the men of the Quorum of Twelve Apostles. Furthermore, the Church of Christ's relationship with the RLDS Church, as well as with other branches or divisions of the Restoration, would be directly affected. On April 10, 1928, the *Independence Examiner* carried a front-page article titled: "Temple by Revelation." That same day the *Kansas City Times* carried a similar article titled: "Divine Edict to Build: Church of Christ Conference Accepts Temple 'Revelation.'"[10]

At the April 11th session of the 1928 conference, "in harmony with the manifestation given through Clarence L. Wheaton, which was approved by the Quorum of Twelve" a committee of three was blessed and set apart for "the reception of divine instruction in regard to the plans for the Temple." Those selected were Otto Fetting, Walter L. Gates and Thomas B. Nerrin.[11] The *Independence Examiner* dutifully reported on April 12, 1928,

---

[8] To All Divisions of the Church of the Restoration (Independence, Missouri: Church of Christ, 1931), 1-4, Miscellaneous Pamphlet Collection, Community of Christ Library-Archives, Independence, Missouri. This letter or epistle consists of four printed pages and is in a pamphlet format. See also "To All Divisions of the Church of the Restoration and to All People in All Lands and Countries Who Believe in God the Eternal Father and in Jesus Christ His Son," *Zion's Advocate* 8, no. 16 (August 15, 1931): 121-2.

[9] "Temple by Revelation: Church of Christ General Conference Receives What is Considers [sic] a Divine Command to Build," *Independence Examiner*, April 10, 1928, 1.

[10] Ibid.; "A Divine Edict to Build: Church of Christ Conference Accepts Temple 'Revelation,'" *Kansas City Times* (April 10, 1928), 1.

[11] "The General Conference of 1928," *Zion's Advocate* 5, no. 5 (May 1928): 66.

that the Church of Christ had "selected the three men who are to have charge of the building of the proposed temple there."[12]

Preparation to commence construction of the temple in 1929 was slow but steady. The July 1928 edition of *Zion's Advocate* published a seven-verse poem written by Nelda Inslee titled: "Build The Temple." The first four lines of verse two captured the enthusiasm of the "just concluded" conference and the anticipation of the commencement of the long-awaited "temple building project." It read:

> Build the Temple, do not tarry,
> For the time's not far away
> When the Lord must find His temple,
> In this time, — the Latter Day.[13]

On October 24, 1928, Apostle Clarence L. Wheaton wrote to the "Committee on Plans for the Temple." In paragraph two of his letter he conveyed to the "Committee" that:

> I have received to my own satisfaction the witness of the Spirit of the divinity of the Message received on September 1st, 1928, ["Sixth Message"][14] which has been confirmed again and again as I have refer[r]ed to it in sermons.[15]

According to an article in the *Independence Examiner*, Wheaton had announced, during the previous April (1928) conference that he, too, had had a revelatory experience wherein he was told that the church was to have "three men to take

---

[12] "Incorporate Church: Decision at Church of Christ Conference Today," *Independence Examiner*, April 12, 1928, 3.

[13] Nelda Inslee, "Build the Temple," *Zion's Advocate* 5, no. 7 (July 1928): 109.

[14] *Word of the Lord*, 16-20. The "Sixth Message" was received at Fetting's home in Port Huron, Michigan, on September 1, 1928.

[15] Clarence L. Wheaton, Letter to Committee on Plans for the Temple, October 24, 1928. Photocopy in possession of the author.

charge of the temple project, formulating plans and executing them."[16]

While much instruction regarding building particulars was conveyed in the "Sixth Message," verse 10 also carried a warning that: "Many will believe it, but some will reject it, because darkness has clouded their minds."[17] The "Committee" addressed a letter to the "Quorum of Twelve" dated October 8, 1928, and mailed from Port Huron, Michigan. The letter made several specific proposals regarding the preparation for building the temple and also included a typed copy of the "Sixth Message."[18] In responding to Fetting, certain of the apostles relayed their concern over developing opposition by some members of the church (which Apostle Thomas J. Sheldon hinted at). Apostle Bert C. Flint was more direct when he stated in his October 11, 1928, letter to the committee: "WE ARE EXPERIENCING OPPOSITION already from some who have been, and should now be our loyal supporters and assistants. There seems to be developing an organized opposition among us to the idea of Temple building."[19]

Bishop William P. Buckley, in a response written on October 14, 1928, and addressed to Otto Fetting remarked: "There may be adverse conditions to face from some. Opposition by some who would be assistants instead of deterants [sic]."[20] Apostle Elmer E. Long in his letter to Otto Fetting dated October 16, 1928, also remarked: "Satan [is] alert and will, no doubt, increase his efforts to hinder. I expect to see the opposition institute legal

---

[16] "Temple Lot History: Apostle Clarence L. Wheaton, in Sermon Last Night, Digs Deeply into Past of Famous Tract," *Independence Examiner*, April 28, 1928.

[17] *Word of the Lord*, 16-20.

[18] Otto Fetting, Walter L. Gates, and Thomas B. Nerren, Letter to the Quorum of Twelve, October 8, 1928. Photocopy in possession of the author.

[19] Bert C. Flint, Letter to Otto Fetting, Walter L. Gates, and Thomas B. Nerren, October 11, 1928. Capitalization in original letter. Photocopy in possession of the author.

[20] William P. Buckley, Letter to Otto Fetting, October 14, 1928. Photocopy in possession of the author.

proceedings when we start to mote [move] dirt, if not before. I have felt that for some weeks."[21] Finally, Apostle Wheaton, in concluding his response to the "Committee on Plans for the Temple" commented: "As General church officials we should do all in our power to avert a crisis between contending forces at the 1929 conference."[22]

One of the particulars conveyed in his letter to his fellow apostles, Fetting suggested that stakes to mark the four corners of the proposed temple be set in accordance with the previously announced dimensions: 90 feet by 180 feet.[23] This suggestion did not, however, meet with unanimous approval. Apostle Hiram E. Moler wrote back to Fetting: "it seems to me that it would be pre-mature to attempt to locate the site of the Temple at this time, or at any time prior to The General Conference taking action on your report."[24] Apostle Thomas J. Sheldon queried:

> If we drive temporary stakes now it will in a way commit the church to the size of the temple before the Church has adopted the report of the committee...If it should be later discovered that Joseph [meaning Joseph Smith Jr.] located the northeast corner in a little different place than we select; or if you as the committee receive definite instruction concerning the exact location that might differ to any extent from the temporary markers, it would place us in an embarassing [sic] position before our enemies to explain the change.[25]

Clearly everyone within the church did not share the excitement of the proposed temple and the matter of setting

---

[21] Elmer E. Long, Letter to Otto Fetting, October 16, 1928. Photocopy in possession of the author.

[22] Clarence L. Wheaton, letter to the "Committee on Plans for the Temple," October 24, 1928. Photocopy in possession of the author.

[23] *Word of the Lord*: 17.

[24] Hiram E. Moler, extract of letter to Otto Fetting and/or Committee on Plans for the Temple, October 17, 1928. Photocopy in possession of the author.

[25] Thomas J. Sheldon, Letter to Committee on Plans for the Temple, October 16, 1928. The mention of "Joseph" by Sheldon in this quote most certainly refers to the Prophet Joseph Smith. Photocopy in possession of the author.

stakes pre-maturely was an item of concern and disagreement even among the apostles. Notwithstanding these concerns and counsel to the contrary, Fetting had his way and the stakes were set for the temple according to the dimensions prescribed.[26]

On November 4, 1928, *the Kansas City Star* featured an article titled: "A Mormon Temple Start — Stakes Set at Independence for Building in 1929." The sub-heading read: "Another Divine Message Directing the Construction Is Reported, While Aid in Funds Is Assured." In discussing the event, the article continued:

> Stakes were set in the famous Temple Lot at Independence late yesterday to indicate the exact site of a temple which is being projected by the Church of Christ, a Mormon sect which owns the ground.

The article quoted Walter L. Gates, who stated:

> Brother Fetting has assured us that on last Tuesday the same divine messenger appeared to him and talked to him further of the details of the proposed temple. We are having calls from people in various parts of the world who are intensely interested in the enterprise and who have assured us they will help finance it.[27]

With the stakes set, the church was ready to proceed with the actual building of the temple — appointed for the year 1929. During the previous October, the idea of "turning sod" on April 6, 1929, as part of the annual conference of the church was also discussed between Apostles Fetting and Sheldon.[28] On October 16, 1928, Apostle Sheldon had suggested that "it would be very fine to designate the temple site during conference, as there will be saints who would desire to witness the scene and they would

---

[26] "Choose Site for Temple: Church of Christ Building Committee Set Stakes for House It Says God Commanded It to Build," *Independence Examiner*, November 5, 1928.

[27] "A Mormon Temple Start: Stakes Set at Independence for Building in 1929," *Kansas City Star*, November 4, 1928.

[28] Otto Fetting, Letter to Thomas J. Sheldon, October 19, 1928. Photocopy in possession of the author.

tell it to their children and grandchildren as one of the most important events that has transpired in this generation."[29]

Fetting responded on October 19th and indicated that "at the conference of 1929...all probabilities are that the first sod will be turned for the building of the sacred structure, the Temple upon the Temple Lot."[30] A week later Fetting again responded to another Sheldon letter (apparently no longer extant) wherein he stated: "Your suggestion in your last letter as to turning the first sod at the next Conference [April 1929] for the Temple is a good one and it will bring a big crowd to Conference."[31] Accordingly, a ground-breaking or "turning the first sod" ceremony was planned for the next conference of the church. The opening session, followed by the ground-breaking ceremony in the afternoon, was set for April 6, 1929, which conveniently fell on a Saturday.[32]

Shortly after this round of correspondence between Fetting, the "Committee," and the individual apostles, Fetting received his "Seventh and Eighth Messages" on October 30, 1928, and November 30, 1928, respectively.[33] The "Ninth Message" was received on March 8, 1929, and the "Tenth Message" on March 23, 1929, approximately two weeks prior to the historic conference scheduled for April 6, 1929.[34] All four of these

[29] Thomas J. Sheldon, Letter to Committee on Plans for the Temple, October 16, 1928. Photocopy in possession of the author.

[30] Otto Fetting, Letter to Thomas J. Sheldon, October 19, 1928. Photocopy in possession of the author.

[31] Otto Fetting, Letter to Thomas J. Sheldon, October 25, 1928. Photocopy in possession of the author.

[32] "Break Ground for Temple: Long-Looked-For Event to Take Place at 2 p.m. Tomorrow," *Independence Examiner*, April 5, 1929, 1; "The Marking of an Epoch," *Zion's Advocate* (Special Temple Number) 6, no. 5 (May 1929): 56.

[33] *Word of the Lord*, 20-22. The "Seventh Message" was received at Fetting's home in Port Huron, Michigan, on October 30, 1928. The "Eighth Message" was received at Fetting's home in Port Huron, Michigan, on November 30, 1928.

[34] "Break Ground for Temple: Long-Looked-For Event to Take Place at 2 p.m. Tomorrow," *Independence Examiner*, April 5, 1929; "Church Group to Receive 'Divine' Plan for Temple: Trio to Tell Quorum of 'God's Will' for Structure," *Kansas*

"Messages" provided more detail regarding the construction of the temple. The particulars were often extremely detailed which included materials, room dimensions, thickness of walls, number of pillars, etc. The "Tenth Message," verses 2 and 4, are excellent examples of that detail described by the "Messenger." They read, in part:

> Verse 2 — Let the pillars go to the rock and the columns be three feet through and those that are on the side shall be cut in two; but let the pillars go to the rock. Let there be twelve windows on the north and twelve windows on the south, and let there be a division at the top and tied with steel that the walls may be strong for storms shall come that shall test the workmanship that you shall do.
>
> Verse 4 — Let the building be tied with steel at the dividing of the inner court which shall be sixty-five feet from north to south, and fifty-five feet from east to west. Let there be an archway between the outer and the inner court, the details of which I will give you later."[35]

In addition, the "Tenth Message" also specifically instructed Fetting and the church that the stakes as set on November 3, 1928,[36] were not where they should be. Verse 2 began: "The building that you have staked is set ten feet too far to the east and if you will move the stakes then it shall stand upon the place that has been pointed out by the finger of God."[37] The stakes were "re-set" in accordance with the "Messenger's" instructions prior to the commencement of the ground-breaking ceremony set for April 6, 1929.[38] Apostle Daniel Macgregor composed a

---

City Journal-Post, April 4, 1929; *Word of the Lord*, 23-24 and 25-26. The "Ninth Message" was received at Fetting's home in Port Huron, Michigan, on March 8, 1929. The "Tenth Message" was received on March 23, 1929 (no location given).

[35] *Word of the Lord*, 25.

[36] "Choose Site for Temple: Church of Christ Building Committee Set Stakes for House It Says God Commanded It to Build," *Independence Examiner*, November 4, 1928; "A Mormon Temple Start: Stakes Set at Independence for Building in 1929," *Kansas City Star*, November 5, 1928.

[37] *Word of the Lord*, 25.

[38] Elmer E. Long, "The *Stone* Which the *Builders* Rejected," *Zion's Advocate* 6, no. 6 (June 1929): 69. Italics in original; *Word of the Lord*, 25.

poem capturing the feelings of the members of the church as they anxiously awaited the ground-breaking ceremony:

THE TEMPLE LOT

Its [sic] only an old piece of turf
Triangular, sodded and high
But God hath decreed it sacred
And He who hath spake cannot lie.
Tis only of commonplace soil
From whence human bodies have come;
But there shall the Temple of God
Arise shining forth as the sun.

And now that the day of the Lord
Is dawning to bless all the earth
We'll turn to the blessed Temple Lot
From whence an Endowment goes forth.
United, enlightened, empowered,
God's servants to Israel shall turn.
Oh, then shall the Lamanite bands
Rejoice, and our hearts within burn.[39]

With the re-staking completed, final preparation was rushed toward the anticipated ground-breaking ceremony. In its March 1929 issue, the editor of *Zion's Advocate* announced that "Apostle Otto Fetting is of the opinion that the turning of the sod as a beginning of the Temple work should begin on the afternoon of April 6th, the first day of our next General Conference."[40]

---

[39] Daniel Macgregor, "The Temple Lot," *Zion's Advocate* 6, no. 4 (April 1929), 50. First and third verses shown.

[40] "Editorial Items," *Zion's Advocate* 6, no. 3 (March 1929), 34.

Turning the "First Sod" for the Temple

I N ACCORDANCE WITH the specific year (1929) as seen in vision by Apostle Fetting in 1928 and as cited in the "Fifth Message," the Church of Christ held an impressive ground breaking ceremony as scheduled on Saturday, April 6, 1929, in conjunction with the annual conference of the church.[1] *Zion's Advocate* reported:

> From far and near the delegates and visitors assembled in the church on the Temple Lot, taxing its seating capacity to the limit, for the word had gone forth that a thing was to be done which patriarchs and prophets had longed to see, and which would never occur again, namely: the breaking of the sod for the Temple which the prophets have declared would be reared in this generation, and wherein Christ is to meet His people when He comes again.[2]

At the appointed time, a large crowd of 200 to 300 faithful saints and curious outsiders assembled about 100 feet south of the meeting house. The weather was considered favorable for an early April outdoor gathering.[3] After "appropriate songs,

---

[1] Julius C. Billeter, *The Temple of Promise: Jackson County, Missouri*, (Independence, Missouri: Zion's Printing and Press Company, 1946), 139 (hereafter cited as Billeter, *Temple of Promise*); "Sacred Soil Broken for the New Temple: Bishop Frisbey Sinks the Spade into the Tough Sod While Multitude Looks On," *Independence Examiner*, April 8, 1929, 1.

[2] "The Marking of an Epoch," *Zion's Advocate* 6, no. 5 (Special Temple Number) (May 1929): 56.

[3] Ibid., 61; Billeter, *Temple of Promise*, 139.

Members of the Church of Christ assembled for the ground-breaking ceremony of the proposed temple, April 6, 1929, CHURCH OF CHRIST (TEMPLE LOT)

sermons, prayers, and scripture reading, Bishop A[lma] O. Frisbey 'took the spade and cut out and laid upon the ground a small square of sod.'"[4]

The *Independence Examiner* reported the event on the Monday following, April 8, 1929. It was a front-page story with the bold headline: "Sacred Soil Broken for the New Temple: Bishop Frisbey Sinks the Spade into the Tough Sod While Multitude Looks On." The article began: "In the presence of a large and intensely-interested crowd, A[lma] O. Frisbey, bishop of the Church of Christ, at 3 [2] o'clock Saturday afternoon broke the sod on the Temple Lot, the first step in the construction

---

[4] Billeter, *Temple of Promise*, 139; "The Marking of an Epoch," *Zion's Advocate* 6, no. 5 (Special Temple Number) (May 1929): 56; Flint, *An Outline History of the Church of Christ*, 141; *Program for the Breaking of the Ground for the Temple*, Church of Christ, Independence, Missouri, April 6, 1929. Copy of the *Program* provided to the author by Geri Adams, Blue Springs, Missouri. Adams is a great, great granddaughter of Granville Hedrick.

Church of Christ Bishop Alma O. Frisbey ready to lift out the first square of sod at the April 6, 1929, ground-breaking ceremony, CHURCH OF CHRIST (TEMPLE LOT)

of the proposed new temple."[5] Excavation commenced in late April 1929.[6]

The Church of Christ issued a "Special Temple Number" for its May 1929 edition of *Zion's Advocate.*[7] As might be expected the newspaper carried the details of the prayers, speeches and scripture readings together with photos taken at the event.

Another item of importance that was transacted at the April conference was the choosing of five men to compose the

[5] "Sacred Soil Broken for the New Temple: Bishop Frisbey Sinks the Spade into the Tough Sod While Multitude Looks On," *Independence Examiner*, April 8, 1929, 1.

[6] "Clearing the Temple Lot: Trees Being Removed from Temple Site," *Independence Examiner*, April 26, 1929; Billeter, *Temple of Promise*, 139."

[7] *Zion's Advocate* 6, no. 5 (Special Temple Number) (May 1929). The May issue had an additional two-page cover preceding the regular periodical titled: "Special Temple Number." It featured a panoramic photo of the large crowd assembled for the ground-breaking service of April 6, 1929. A second photo featured the three members of the "Temple Plans Committee" (left to right: Walter L. Gates, Otto Fetting, Thomas R. Nerren) and Bishop Alma O. Frisbey (holding the spade with which he "broke sod").

Church of Christ (Temple Lot) Bishop Alma O. Frisbey holding historic stone from excavation of temple site. RLDS Church Apostle Joseph Luff looks on, May-June 1929, COMMUNITY OF CHRIST LIBRARY-ARCHIVES

"Temple Building Committee." Those chosen were: "Henry H. Johnson, Cameron, Mo.; R[ichard] M. Maloney, Oklahoma City, Ok.; J[ames] G. Pointer, Independence, Mo.; Thomas B. Nerrin, Denver, Colo.; W[illiam] P. Buckley, Independence."[8]

The *Independence Examiner* carried a front-page story on April 10, 1929, wherein it announced: "Building Committee: Church of Christ Conference Adopts Quorum of Twelve Recommendation over Objection." The objection was from Marshall T. Jamison and was in the form of a motion. He moved: "that inasmuch as the plans for the building of the temple were from God, as the conference had agreed, why not wait and ask the Lord to indicate who should serve as architect and superintendent of construction." Elmer E. Long responded that "the Lord already had done as much as the conference had any right to expect, and that the Quorum of

---

[8] "The Temple Building Committee," *Zion's Advocate* 6, no. 5 (May 1929): 62; "Five Men are Chosen To Build the Temple," *Independence Examiner* (April 13, 1929), 1.

Historic stone found May 18, 1929, while excavating for the temple foundation. The stone is displayed at Church of Christ (Temple Lot) Visitors Center, Independence, BILL CURTIS

Twelve's recommendation should be adopted as presented."[9] The Jamison amendment was not accepted and the Quorum of Twelve "proposal was adopted as presented." At this time (statement issued at the April conference) the Temple Fund had a total of $889.00.[10]

This bold step toward fulfilling Joseph Smith Jr.'s long-awaited prophecy must have been difficult for RLDS Church members, especially since perhaps as many one thousand former

---

[9] "Building Committee: Church of Christ Conference Adopts Quorum of Twelve Recommendation over Objection," *Independence Examiner* (April 10, 1929), 1.

[10] "Audited Report of Bishop's Books: For Conference Year, April 4, 1928, to March 15, 1929," *Zion's Advocate* 6, no. 6 (June 1929): 83.

members had affiliated with the Church of Church by 1929.[11] At this point, the Temple Lot property owned by the Church of Christ officially comprised 2.75 acres.[12] On April 7, the previous day's groundbreaking was undoubtedly on the minds of many of those in attendance at the Sunday communion service in the RLDS Stone Church (located across the street from the Temple Lot). Elbert A. Smith, a counselor in Frederick M. Smith's First Presidency, gave an "inspired statement" concerning the temple:

> I have gathered my people out from the world, saith the Lord, even from many different parts of the earth, and you are here as seed to be planted in my fields of Zion, and if you will be faithful and humble and consecrate yourselves the harvest shall be very great and very beautiful.
>
> In one of the darkest hours I gave the promise to my people, Zion shall not be moved out of her place, notwithstanding her children are scattered...to build up the waste places of Zion.
>
> Be not troubled in your minds by anything that shall occur. Mark this well: I say unto you, The only temple standing on earth today built by commandment of heaven is in your possession (the Kirtland Temple)...and when the time shall come, in my way, and in my hour, and in my manner...I will command you further concerning the building of my temple in Zion.[13]

---

[11] Flint, *An Outline History of the Church of Christ*, 139, 142, claimed 4,000 members in October 1929, but Ronald E. Romig, Community of Christ archivist, email to R. Jean Addams, March 6, 2009, concluded that the maximum number of transfers to the Church of Christ in the 1920s and 1930s was 1,500. My own estimate is between 1,250 and 1,600 transfers during 1916–36. Statistical data are available in the following sources: "Church of Christ Meets," *Independence Examiner*, April 7, 1928 (provides 1928 church membership data); Clarence L. Wheaton, "Delegates or Referendum," *Zion's Advocate* 6, no. 9 (September 1929): 129 (provides 1929 church membership data).

[12] On July 17, 1906, the City of Independence sold Richard E. Hill, acting as trustee-in-trust for the Church of Christ, a small, triangular strip of land (approximately .25 acre) lying just north of the 2.5 acres the Church already owned. He paid $75. The small triangle had originally been platted as part of a street that was abandoned by the city. Jackson County, Property Records, City of Independence to Richard Hill, July 17, 1906, 264:621–22.

[13] *History of the RLDS Church*, vol. 8, 102-03.

Second stone uncovered June 26, 1929, while excavating for temple foundation. Church of Christ (Temple Lot) officials believe that inscription stands for South East Corner Temple 1831, ALEX BAUGH

The RLDS Church wasted "no time" in getting out their message following the "ground-breaking" ceremony of April 6, 1929. Following up on the April 7th revelation to President Elbert A. Smith, RLDS Church Apostle J. Franklin Curtis produced a 63 page pamphlet in June of 1929, titled: *The Temple of the Lord; Who Shall Build It?* It was published by the RLDS Church owned Herald Publishing House. It immediately set about to examine the claims of the Church of Christ, including a rehash of the same subjects (and not necessarily related to the temple) argued over for many years past. The Curtis pamphlet questioned "the spot," Otto Fetting's "Messages," Granville Hedrick as a prophet, those who had defected from the RLDS Church, etc.[14]

However, the distractions posed by the RLDS Church did not hamper the commencement of the building of the temple. The *Torch of Truth* carried an article in its June 1929 publication which discussed the "active preparation for construction work on the Temple."[15] The editor mentioned that:

> A house has been purchased on Lexington Street a short distance from the Temple Lot and is being fitted up for a boarding and lodging house for the workers who come to labor on the Temple.[16]

Simultaneously to the acquisition of the boarding house, the site for the temple was being cleared of the trees planted by faithful saints nearly a half-century before. The *Independence Examiner* featured a story on April 26, 1929, headed: "Clearing Temple Lot: Trees Being Removed from Temple Site."[17] A

[14] J. Franklin Curtis, *The Temple of the Lord; Who Shall Build It?* (Independence, Missouri: Herald Publishing House, 1929).

[15] James E. Yates, "Active Preparation for Building the Temple," *Torch of Truth* 4, no. 5 (June 1929): 45; "From the Building Committee," *Zion's Advocate* 6, no. 6 (June 1929): 73.

[16] James E. Yates, "Active Preparation for Building the Temple," *Torch of Truth* 4, no. 5 (June 1929): 45.

[17] "Clearing Temple Lot: Trees Being Removed from Temple Site — Wood Will be Used in Making Furniture," *Independence Examiner*, April 26, 1929; "From the

total of twelve trees, planted by church members fifty or more years previous, were removed from the excavation site. James R. Lawson, project manager, was quoted as saying: "'the ash trees...are to be rough sawed and dry kilned to furnish some of the material for the building of the furniture and perhaps a part of the altar of the new temple.'"[18]

The actual excavation began as soon as the trees had been removed and the brush cleared from the site. Soon thereafter, on April 30, 1929, Apostle Otto Fetting received the "Eleventh Message." Once again, he was told that the project was to be pushed forward. Additional instructions and temple description details were also revealed.[19]

On May 18, 1929, soon after the actual digging had begun, Harry Taylor "was operating a slip drawn by a team of horses, [when] the implement came in contact with a hard object which suddenly stopped the team. Hastily digging into the loose black soil, Lawson and others uncovered a block of limestone of ordinary native variety." The stone was approximately ten and one half inches square and seven inches thick. On one side of the stone "was what appeared to be lettering which had been chiselled [sic] into the stone." The reporter indicated:

> The figures 1831 were fairly readable. This was the year in which Joseph Smith [Jr.] dedicated the temple lot and set the corner stone. The other lettering was not so legible, but today it was announced that it had been deciphered as 40 W. This was construed to mean 40 West.[20]

Building Committee," *Zion's Advocate* 6, no. 6 (June 1929): 73.

[18] "Clearing Temple Lot: Trees Being Removed from Temple Site — Wood Will be Used in Making Furniture," *Independence Examiner*, April 26, 1929.

[19] *Word of the Lord*, 26-29. The "Eleventh Message" was received on April 30, 1929 (no location given).

[20] "Find Historic Stone Upon the Temple Lot: Believed by Church of Christ Officials to be One Set There by Mormon Prophet," *Independence Examiner*, May 29, 1929, 1; Elmer E. Long, "The *Stone* Which the *Builders* Rejected," *Zion's Advocate* 6, no. 6 (June 1929): 69.

The *Kansas City Star* on May 29, 1929, reported: "Divine revelation has been bolstered at the Temple lot...where ...the Church of Christ is excavating for the temple." The article continued:

> They have uncovered a stone, a battered, earthworn stone with faint ciphering on it, which the seers of the church today pronounced as the original cornerstone laid by Joseph Smith on the temple lot in 1831, and which they regarded as confirmation as divine and infallible the revelation made by an angel to Otto Fetting...a year and a half ago as to the proper site for the temple.[21]

With the inherent publicity that soon accompanied this find, officials of the Church of Christ announced through the local press (*Independence Examiner*) that:

> "The stone is in the custody of Bishop A[lma] O. Frisbey, and he will take no chances on it," Elder [William P.] Buckley said, today. "He is going to have a strong box made as a receptacle of the sacred relic, and provided with [a] heavy plate glass over it, so that visitors may see the stone, but will not be allowed to handle it."[22]

In the same article the *Independence Examiner* announced the opening of the Temple Café at 827 West Lexington Street "in a new building." The article further noted: "The café is in charge of Miss Alta Case, who operates it for the church, and any profits that accrue from it are to go to the Temple building fund."[23]

The Church of Christ immediately trumpeted the "find" and the importance of the "stone." The headline of the June

---

[21] "Find 1831 Temple Site: Stone Uncovered at Independence is 'Hailed By Saints,'" *Kansas City Star*, May 29, 1929.

[22] "Safety for the Stone: Sacred Marker Found on Temple Lot to be Placed under Heavy Glass in a Box," *Independence Examiner*, May 31, 1929.

[23] Ibid.

1929 publication of *Zion's Advocate* boldly declared: "The *Stone* Which the *Builders* Rejected."[24]

No sooner had the excitement from the unearthing of the first stone quieted down, when a second stone was discovered in much the same way, by the same persons, on June 26, 1929. The *Kansas City Star* announced: "A Second Temple Stone: '1831' Inscribed on a Slab Found at Independence."[25] The stone was found under about eighteen inches of dirt near the south side of the excavation site. It was very similar to the first stone found about six weeks earlier, i.e., "native limestone, six inches thick, ten inches wide and about twelve inches long."[26] The *Independence Examiner* reported the discovery with a headline inquiry: "Is This a Sacred Stone?" Of the second stone they reported: "On one side of it easily could be read the numerals, 1831. Other characters had been chiselled upon the stone, but they were indistinct. They looked like the capital letters S E C T." These letters were interpreted to mean "South East Corner Temple."[27]

Meanwhile, the excavation for the temple continued. The *Independence Examiner* reported that "at present sixteen men are working on the job, who have been sent from various churches over the country to labor here on this project."[28] The article quoted William P. Buckley (secretary of the building committee and a bishop in the church) as saying: "'daily subscriptions of money are arriving in the mails from all over the country... besides supplies such as bedding and other items.'" Of particular interest, the article also commented: "The construction project

---

[24] Elmer E. Long, "The *Stone* Which the *Builders* Rejected," *Zion's Advocate* 6, no. 6 (June 1929): 69. Italics in original.

[25] "A Second Temple Stone: '1831' Inscribed on a Slab Found at Independence," *Kansas City Star*, June 27, 1929.

[26] Ibid.

[27] "Is This a Sacred Stone?: Church of Christ Interested in Find of Excavators," *Independence Examiner*, June 27, 1929. Underscore of capital letters by author.

[28] "For the New Temple: Additional Details of Plans Being Revealed from Time to Time by Angelic Visitor, Fetting Says," *Independence Examiner*, August 8, 1929.

is very much out of the ordinary in that the complete plans are not available. The plans are being drawn a part at a time by Fred H. Bartlett of Denver under the direction of Otto Fetting of Port Huron, Mich., who declares that a messenger from the Lord comes from time to time revealing the divine requirements for this building as details are needed on the job."[29]

Funds to keep the excavation and foundation portion of the temple project moving forward were, of course, desperately needed. This required a constant effort by church officials. In the August 1929 issue, *Zion's Advocate* featured a "Circular Letter" dated July 1, 1929. It was addressed: "To All the Saints and Those Who Are Interested in the Building of the Temple." William P. Buckley, secretary of the "Building Committee" authored the epistle.[30] He began his request by stating that "the excavation for the basement is nearly completed and we are ready now to begin the trenching for the walls, which are to go down to the rock." (Buckley's statement was overly optimistic.) He then stated the "Committee's" specific appeal:

> All those who want to donate their time and labor in this work, send us your names and information at once. We want 50 men.
>
> Those who cannot assist by your labor, will you now assist by sending in your contributions for this part of the work? It will take approximately Twenty-Five Thousand Dollars ($25,000) for the trenches, in cribbing, and for the concrete and steel for these basement walls and floor fabrication. We want to see this part of the work finished by the first of next November; and we must have your help to enable us to do it.[31]

---

[29] Ibid.

[30] William P. Buckley, "Circular Letter from the Temple Building Committee," *Zion's Advocate* 6, no. 8 (August 1929): 105. The Buckley letter (Buckley was one of the seven bishops of the church) was addressed: "To All the Saints and Those Who Are Interested in the Building of the Temple," and was a reprint of a letter apparently sent to the various churches of the Restoration on July 1, 1929, by the "Temple Building Committee at Independence, Missouri."

[31] Ibid.

A Call to All Branches of the Restoration

BEGINNING IN JULY 1928, after the memorable conference of April 1928 (when Otto Fetting's "Message 5" was read to and accepted by the church), the Church of Christ went on record and stated that they were to "take the lead"[1] in the construction of the temple. This statement, however, left open the possibility and, in fact, the need to solicit financial support from other divisions of the "Restoration."

Approximately ten months prior to the April 1929 conference of the Church of Christ, Apostle Clarence L. Wheaton traveled to Salt Lake City, Utah, and met with officials of the LDS Church, and, in particular, President Heber J. Grant "who made them feel welcome on a tour of the city."[2] The *Messenger* reported somewhat later, but undoubtedly referring to the same trip, that Wheaton was "royally entertained by a Utah dignitary."[3] In November 1928, Apostle James E. Yates of the Church of Christ traveled to Salt Lake City and also met with LDS President Heber J. Grant "soliciting fraternal support."[4] The *Messenger*, in its February 1929 issue, remarked:

[1] Hiram E. Moler, "The General Conference of 1928," *Zion's Advocate* 5, no. 7 (July 1928): 98.

[2] "Clipping from Oneida County Enterprise," *Torch of Truth* 3, no. 7 (July 1928): 88. The *Oneida Enterprise* was published in Malad, Idaho (1923–1930).

[3] T. M. Irvine, "More About Temple Building," *Messenger* 5, no. 2 (February 1929): 12.

[4] "Apostle Yates Speaks: Members of Church of Christ on Temple Lot, in Utah," *Independence Examiner*, November 21, 1928.

Temple Lot excavation. Basement for temple nearly completed. C. Ed Miller photograph, Church of Christ (Temple Lot)

It is undoubtedly true that the Utah Church has ample funds, if so disposed, to finance the building of the proposed temple in Independence....It, undoubtedly, would be quite a help to them [the Church of Christ] if the Utah leaders would finance the temple project of the Church of Christ. Will these 'apostles' [the Church of Christ] overlook polygamy... and blood atonement as taught by early leaders in order to have the support of the Utah Church? And will the members of the Church of Christ stand for any such purpose? We will wait and see.[5]

The Church of Christ was well aware of the questioning and negative comments made by those of other branches of the "Restoration," besides the RLDS Church which had already made their position amply clear. The August 1929 publication of *Zion's Advocate* noted in its lead article several critical remarks made by certain individuals:

[5] T. M. Irvine, "More About Temple Building," *Messenger* 5, no. 2 (February 1929): 12.

The command to build the Temple and the ready response of the Church of Christ to assume the task has caused a great flurry among the factional leaders of Mormonism. At first the matter was treated with haughty contempt, one business man expressing himself thus: 'The Hedrickites have neither money nor intelligence enough to build the Temple,' while a prominent official in Utah said: 'They can not build a temple, for they do not know how, nor do they know for what a Temple is to be used.' And still another: A well known sister in Independence met an elder of the Church of Christ and mirthfully asked: 'Have you got money enough to build the Temple?'[6]

Notwithstanding the criticism being leveled against them, the apostles of the Church of Christ again began to aggressively solicit construction funds from all "branches" of the Restoration, including the RLDS and LDS Churches.

At the October 6, 1929, morning conference session of the LDS Church in Salt Lake City, Utah, President Anthony W. Ivins of the First Presidency addressed the matter of the solicitation for funds for the Independence temple by the elders of the Church of Christ. He remarked:

It is a well known fact to many of you that these people have sent out their agents, who have recently visited many of the wards of the Church in the stakes of Zion that are in Utah, Arizona, California, Idaho[,] and in other places. The message which they bring us is this: that the Lord has revealed to them that the time has come when the temple is to be erected upon the temple lot at Jackson county, that this scripture which I have read, from [S]ection 84 of the Doctrine and Covenants, may be fulfilled, because they call attention to the fact that the generation which lived at the time that the revelation was given has about passed away.

He continued:

They have been to us. They have come to our office, soliciting aid. They would like us to assist them in building a temple…It is true that a house may be erected upon that tract of ground in this generation, but

---

[6] "The Way of *Law* and *Order*," *Zion's Advocate* 6, no. 8 (August 1929): 101. Italics in the original.

it will not be a temple erected to the name of the Lord and accepted by him, until the time comes when he shall speak through the proper channel, and the work be accomplished by his recognized church.[7]

Following his address, President Charles W. Nibley, also of the LDS Church First Presidency, reiterated what Ivins had said and added: "Do not allow this question of the building of the temple in Jackson County [to] worry you."[8] Also speaking at the Sunday morning session was Rudger Clawson, president of the LDS Church's Quorum of Twelve Apostles. He also addressed this subject. He quoted Ivins' introductory statement "that the time was not ripe for the erection of a Temple at Jackson County, Missouri." He continued by quoting additional comments made earlier by Ivins.[9] Clawson also noted that the Church of Christ had "sought subscription from the Church here to aid the movement; though naturally none was granted" and that "though they are building a structure on the site originally Chosen by the Lord, it will be merely a house rather than a building."[10]

---

[7] *Journal History*, October 6, 1929, 1-3; Church History Library, Salt Lake City, Utah. The clipping was cut from the *Deseret News*, Salt Lake City, Utah, October 7, 1929, and titled: "In the Tabernacle at Salt Lake City, Utah, Sunday, October 6, 1929,".

[8] Ibid., 3-4.

[9] Ibid., 4-5.

[10] Ibid., 4-5.

Building of the Temple Temporarily Suspended— Fracture within the Church

Less than three and one-half months after the excitement of the ground-breaking ceremony and the start of the excavation on the Temple Lot, Apostle Otto Fetting turned the temple building exuberance of the church to one of constraint, bewilderment, and out-right dismay when on July 18, 1929, he received the "Twelfth Message." The "Message" was lengthy and covered a variety of subject matter including: additional instruction regarding the particulars of the temple, a reminder to be actively engaged in missionary work, and the calling of a new apostle to fill a vacancy existing in the quorum. However, it was Verse 4, and Fetting's interpretation of it, that set member against member, and eventually caused a major schism within the ranks of the church. Verse 4 stated:

> Behold, the Lord has rejected all creeds and factions of men, who have gone away from the word of the Lord and have become an abomination in his sight, therefore, let those that come to the Church of Christ be baptized, that they may rid themselves of the traditions and sins of men.[1]

The doctrine construed by Fetting from this verse required all members of the "Mormon" factions, including the RLDS Church, to be "re-baptized" before joining the Church of

---

[1] *Word of the Lord*, 29-33. The "Twelfth Message" was received on July 18, 1929 (no location given).

Christ. Previous to this "introduced" practice, members of other factions of Mormonism could apply for membership based on their former baptism in their previous organization. This arrangement was specifically provided for in the Agreements of Working Harmony. Despite contrary action taken by the RLDS Church in 1926, the Church of Christ had not rescinded the Agreements of Working Harmony and still considered them valid.[2]

Fetting convinced some of the brethren in the leadership of the church, including fellow apostle Walter L. Gates[3] that this matter of "re-baptism" applied to all members, including him, that had "transferred" from the RLDS Church to the Church of Christ. "Re-baptisms" commenced immediately throughout the church without apostolic quorum or church approval.[4] (Formal consent had historically been required on any matter of policy or doctrine, let alone such a major change or adjustment to a specific tenant such as baptism).

A special conference of the church was immediately "called" by members of the Quorum of Twelve Apostles to deal with the "re-baptism" issue.[5] It was scheduled for early October 1929. After several meetings, which extended over several days and which were often very heated and vocal, Fetting and Gates were "silenced for six months" by a vote of the conference 92 to 67 (far from a consensus decision).[6] In a separate motion, pending

---

[2] *History of the RLDS Church*, 8:77.

[3] Gates was ordained an apostle in 1927. He supported Fetting in his position on the issue of "re-baptism" after Fetting's "Twelfth Message" was received on July 18, 1929. He also vocally supported Fetting during the October 1929 "Special Conference."

[4] Thomas W. Williams, "Practice of Rebaptism Stirs the Church of Christ," *Messenger* 5, no. 10 (October 1929): 77; "Apostle Otto Fetting Charged with Heresy: Resolution Asking That He Be Silenced as a Member of Quorum of Twelve Introduced," *Independence Examiner*, October 12, 1929; Flint, *An Outline History of the Church of Christ*, 142.

[5] "General Conference: Church of Christ Opens a Business Session This Afternoon — Much Business Concerning Temple," *Independence Examiner*, October 7, 1929.

[6] "Prophet Fetting Is Out: The Church of Christ 'Silences' Its Visionary," *Kansas City Star*, October 13, 1929; "Silence Otto Fetting: Church of Christ by Vote of 92 to 67,

Marker designating spot where first stone was found, May 18, 1929, R. Jean
Addams

a delegate vote at the April 1930 conference, "re-baptism of
members of the church shall not be taught as a present duty
and shall not be practiced." The conference vote was 110 to 67
(again, far from a consensus).[7] Fetting was also dropped from the
Quorum of Twelve Apostles and Gates was given a six-month
"recess" from the quorum.[8] Over the next two days of meetings,

Adopts Resolution," *Independence Examiner*, October 14, 1929; "Two Dissenters
Accused of Heresy at the Church of Christ Conference," *Kansas City Times*, October
16, 1929; James E. Yates, Clarence L. Wheaton, Arthur M. Smith, Bert C. Flint,
Hiram E. Moler, and Elmer E. Long, "To the Ministry and Membership of the
Church," *Zion's Advocate* 6, no. 11 (November 1929): 149-50.

[7] "Saints Fire on Prophet: Otto Fetting Is Charged with Heresy," *Kansas City Star,*
October 12, 1929; "Silence Otto Fetting: Church of Christ by Vote of 92 to 67,
Adopts Resolution," *Independence Examiner*, October 14, 1929; James E. Yates, et
al., "To the Ministry and Membership of the Church," *Zion's Advocate* 6, no. 11
(November 1929): 149-50; Flint, *Outline History of the Church of Christ*, 142.

[8] "Prophet Fetting Is Out: The Church of Christ 'Silences' Its Visionary," *Kansas
City Star*, October 13, 1929; Elmer E. Long, "Conference Notes," *Zion's Advocate*

other church leaders were also "silenced,"[9] including Thomas B. Nerren (Building Committee), William D. Dexter (General Secretary of the church), and William P. Buckley (secretary of the bishopric and secretary of the "Building Committee").[10]

Fetting would not wait for the results of the referendum. The *Kansas City Times* carried an article on October 15, 1929, reporting that Fetting had refused to be silenced and, in fact, spoke out at a large gathering assembled at the "Church of Jesus Christ, another Mormon faction in Independence" and would "administer the rite [re-baptism] at 2 o'clock Tuesday, making use of the fount [sic] in the Church of Jesus Christ."[11] (This Church of Jesus Christ, led by Benjamin R. MacGuire, was the organization that emerged from the Protest Movement within the RLDS Church against Supreme Directional Control.) Fetting's direct insubordination or disobedience resulted in his being disfellowshipped from the Church of Christ at the April 1930 Conference.[12]

According to Church of Christ Apostle Bert C. Flint, approximately one-third of the total church membership followed Fetting and organized their own church in late 1929 (also called the Church of Christ) with Fetting as their leader.[13]

6, no. 11 (November 1929): 164; J. Franklin Curtis, "The Church of Christ Special Conference," *Herald* 76 (October 23, 1929): 1278-81.

[9] "Silenced Three More High Church Officers: Last Member Temple Plans Committee Displaced by Council of 12," *Independence Examiner*, October 15, 1929; "More Apostles Are Out: Three Followers of Prophet Fetting 'Silenced' by Quorum," *Kansas City Star,* October 15, 1929.

[10] J. Franklin Curtis, "The Church of Christ Special Conference," *Herald* 76, no. 43 (October 23, 1929): 1279. RLDS Church Apostle J. Franklin Curtis attended these stormy sessions and kept copious notes. J. Franklin Curtis, "October 1929 Special Conference of the Church of Christ," J. F. Curtis Collection, P57, f19, Community of Christ Archives-Library, Independence, Missouri.

[11] "Fetting to Carry On: Rebaptism Will Be Administered by Deposed Prophet," *Kansas City Times*, October 15, 1929.

[12] Flint, *An Outline History of the Church of Christ*, 142.

[13] Apostle Bert C. Flint (*An Outline History of the Church of Christ*, 142), stated that the church's membership at the time of the October "Special Conference" approximated

Even among those who remained with the church a feeling of disillusionment was evidenced by the poor showing in the voting for or against the referendum. The official vote, made known to the church prior to the 1930 April conference, was 369 against "re-baptism" and 71 in favor of "re-baptism."[14] As a result of this dissension and the accompanying action taken, the work on the temple project stopped pending further direction.

4000 and that "nearly one-third of the membership" left the church and followed Fetting. The October 1929 membership number, in the author's opinion, (and as stated in a previous footnote dealing with Flint's membership estimate in 1925/1926), is significantly overstated. Likewise, the percentage of those who left the church at this time, in the author's opinion, is high. A more realistic number, for the members who left the church at this time, is between 20% and 25%. Allowing for a continued influx of "transferees" from the RLDS Church between April and October of 1929, the revised Church of Christ membership total, before the Fetting departure, was probably closer to 1500. Finally, the official 1932 membership was reported as 1607. If the defection was 20%, then a revised membership for late 1929/1930 would have been about 1200 after the Fetting-led schism. Again, allowing for continual transfers from the RLDS Church and elsewhere, plus internal growth, the 1932 reported membership of 1607 would be justifiable. Ron Romig, Archivist, Community of Christ (formerly the RLDS Church), after reviewing RLDS Church membership data for this period, concluded that the maximum number of transferees to the Church of Christ in the 1920s and 1930s was 1500 (email to the author dated March 5, 2009). This number concurs with the author's estimate of 1250 to 1600 transferees from the RLDS Church from 1916 to 1936.

[14] "Additional Referendum Votes," *Zion's Advocate* 7, no. 4 (April 1, 1930): 59. The percentage of those voting, after allowing for a one-third depletion (Flint's estimate) in the membership base, was about 47%. If the percentage dropout was 20% (author's estimate) the voting was about 39%.

Efforts to Build the Temple Revived:
Late 1929–1930

S HORTLY AFTER THE CONCLUSION of the special 1929 October
conference, Apostle Clarence L. Wheaton reported:

> I was permitted to have a vision of the Temple, which gave me much
> assurance and has had the effect of lifting to an extent the sadness and
> depression that I have passed through during the last few weeks.

He continued:

> I was taken to the place where the Temple was under construction by
> an individual who remained just a step behind me, who seemed to be
> in charge of the work, and who directed my attention to various parts
> of the work under construction. As we came to the excavation I was
> permitted to inspect the steel that was being placed in position and
> fabricated just as the plans have been given through the Messenger.

As the vision unfolded, Wheaton provided the details. At the
conclusion of his recital he challenged the church as follows:

> Let us move forward. Continue as we have done heretofore and make
> the necessary sacrifices to complete this work. Contribute liberally to
> the Temple Fund.[1]

---

[1] Clarence L. Wheaton, "More Temple Plans Revealed," *Zion's Advocate* 6, no. 11
(November 1929): 53.

This spiritual manifestation to Wheaton greatly diminished the proliferation of rumors that were circulating at this time relative to the Church of Christ rejecting the Fetting "Messages."[2]

No sooner had Wheaton delivered this positive reinforcement to the membership of the church, than insinuations began to be circulated regarding misuse of the temple funds. The *Messenger* reported in December 1929: "Fetting and others in Independence are being sued at law for withholding funds sent in for the temple."[3]

Regardless of the difficulties caused by Fetting and his followers, plans to re-commence the excavation materialized in the winter of 1929–1930. However, frustration from external sources was not over. On February 19, 1930. RLDS Church Apostle Joseph Luff[4] received a revelation which was directed specifically to the Church of Christ. In this communication the Lord stated: "Awake from your delusion, while time is yours... The Temple of your proposing ye shall not be permitted to build as ye have planned."[5] It is a gross "understatement" that the news

---

[2] Thomas W. Williams, "What a Change: Now that Certain Men Are in Power!," *Messenger* 5, no. 12 (December 1929): 100; "The *Church of Christ* in General Conference, 1930," *Zion's Advocate* 7, no. 5 (April 15, 1930): 70. Italics in original.

[3] Thomas W. Williams, "What a Change: Now that Certain Men Are in Power!," *Messenger* 5, no. 12 (December 1929): 100. This matter of litigation was more than "withholding funds." The suit stated the funds had been used for personal gain. The stated amount of damages sought was $338.40. See "Continue Church Caste: More Time in Church of Christ Suit versus Otto Fetting and W[illiam] P. Buckley," *Independence Examiner* (January 6, 1930). On February 12, 1930 a "Judgment was rendered in favor of the Church of Christ." The defendants were required to pay $221.90. See also "Decision for the Church of Christ," *Zion's Advocate* 7 (February 15, 1930): 40.

[4] Joseph Luff was preparing himself for the ministry in the Methodist church when he was introduced to the RLDS Church and baptized in 1876. He changed his vocation to medicine. He was ordained an apostle in 1887 and served in that capacity until 1909 when he was released to be able to devote more time in his additional calling as "Church Physician." His home was located next to the Stone Church in Independence and across the street from the Temple Lot.

[5] Joseph Luff , "Revelation Given to the Church of Christ (Temple Lot)," February 19, 1930, Special Collection, AC 901.A1a no. 4318, Harold B. Lee Library, Brigham

ZION'S ADVOCATE

"And blessed are they who shall seek to bring forth my Zion at that day, for they
shall have the gift and power of the Holy Ghost."—1 Nephi 3:187.

Published Semi Monthly by the Church of Christ

Entered as Second-Class Matter May 14, 1929, at the Post Office at Independence, Mo. under the Act of March 3, 1879"

VOLUME 7	INDEPENDENCE, MISSOURI, NOVEMBER 1, 1930	NUMBER 17

Description of Church of Christ Temple at Independence, Mo.

By Norman L. Wilkinson, Architect

The proposed Temple is to be built upon a practically level site at the southwest corner of the intersection of River Boulevard and Lexington Street in Independence, Missouri. The Temple faces east and consists of a main building ninety feet north to south and one hundred eighty feet east to west. On the east face of the main building is a portico in which are the lobby, stair wells, and open porch.

The porch is floored with marble laid off in patterns, which lead up to the three bronze entrance doors. These doors open into the main lobby, which is decorated with marble tern and walls. The floor being laid out in a Mosaic pattern and the walls being decorated with pilaster panels and entablatures. From this lobby one has access on the north and south to flights of stairs which serve from the lower

Interior View of Main Floor.

"*Let the main floor be used when the Lord's people gather for their general assemblies from time to time, at which times the Lord's Spirit will rest upon them in great power, and will direct them in their work that the Gospel may be preached to all nations in power, for behold your message shall be a message of love, and this power shall come to the servants of the Lord and his people.*"—Fifth Visitation.

The entire exterior of the building is to be faced with a gray polished stone, and to have a curved copper covered roof.

As one approaches the Temple from River Boulevard, he first comes to a broad flight of steps which lead up to a portico of six columns across the front with two columns on each side with a pilaster at the building line.

court to the rooms above the balcony, while on the west side of the lobby are three doors which open into the main room of the Temple of the upper court.

We return now to the exterior view of the Temple. The north and south faces of the Temple are the same: consisting of a series of thirteen engaged columns with twelve of this revelation was not "well received" by the membership of the Church of Christ.

To add to the negative feelings engendered by Luff's revelation, a similar proclamation of doom regarding the erection of the proposed temple was sounded by Apostle Orson F. Whitney of the Church of Jesus Christ of Latter-day Saints in Salt Lake City, Utah. He stated in the June 24, 1930, issue of the *Liahona: The Elders' Journal,* (the missionary periodical of the LDS Church published in Independence, Missouri): "All premature, unauthorized movements in that direction [building of the temple] are fated to end in failure and as the Lord liveth they will come to naught."[6]

Undaunted, the Church of Christ pushed on. In reporting on the April 1930 annual church conference, *Zion's Advocate* announced, in part:

> We feel quite sure the Saints everywhere will be interested in the following action regarding the building of the Temple. In the Eleventh Message it is written: '*The Temple will be built. There will be changes in the men that will help. Those that hinder let them be removed.*' A number *have been removed* whose action '*hindered*' the work.
>
> *Resolved further,* that in the absence of contrary proof we do accept the instructions and specifications in the aforesaid messages pertaining to the building of the Temple, so far as they are found to agree with former revealments, and that we declare it to be our intention to proceed with the construction work as fast as monies come to our hand.[7]

Young University, Provo, Utah. See also: J. F. Curtis Collection, P57, f19, Community of Christ Library-Archives, Independence, Missouri.

[6] Orson F. Whitney, "Zion and Her Stakes," *Liahona: The Elders' Journal* 28, no. 2 (Independence, Missouri: Zion's Printing and Press) (July 8, 1930): 31. The *Liahona: The Elders' Journal* was a publication of the Church of Jesus Christ of Latter-day Saints for all of the missions of the LDS Church in the United States and Canada. Whitney's remarks were first delivered in an address on KSL Radio in Salt Lake City, Utah, Sunday evening, December 1, 1929.

[7] "The Church of Christ in General Conference, 1930," *Zion's Advocate* 7, no. 5 (April 15, 1930): 70.

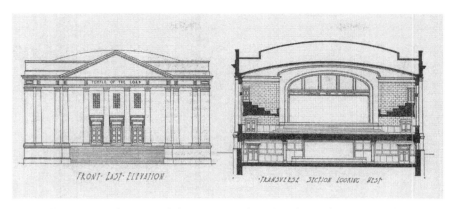

Wilkinson's architectural drawings of the Church of Christ (Temple Lot) proposed temple, 1930. Enhanced by Bill Curtis.

Compounding the pressing issues at hand, i.e., a drop in membership (associated with the defection over the issue of re-baptism) and a desire of the majority of the members of the church to get back to the temple project (coupled with the absolute necessity of raising funds to do so), a move was underway by some in the church to try, again, a cooperative land/farming venture. *Zion's Advocate* carried an article in the June 15, 1930, issue which exhorted the members of the church to participate in just such an undertaking.[8]

Notwithstanding the frustrations and problems the church faced, specific instructions were formulated, soon thereafter, by the Council of Twelve Apostles and presented as a "Recommendation from the Twelve Relative to Resuming Work on the Temple."[9] After discussing the problems and issues of the past it was resolved:

[8] James E. Yates, "Fund Started for Purchase of Land," *Zion's Advocate* 7, no. 9 (June 15, 1930): 103. Also see R. Jean Addams, "The Church of Christ (Temple Lot) and the Law of Consecration," *John Whitmer Historical Association Journal*, (2008), vol. 8, 88-113.

[9] "Recommendation from the Twelve Relative to Resuming Work on the Temple," *Zion's Advocate* 7, no. 5 (April 15, 1930): 74. Beginning with the twentieth century (1926) ordination of apostles in the Church of Christ, the name "Quorum of the

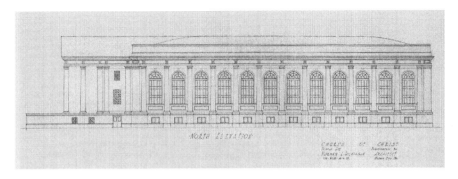

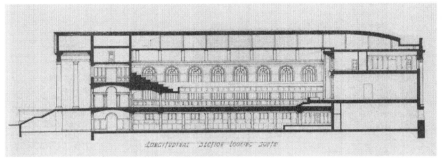

Wilkinson's architectural drawings of the Church of Christ (Temple Lot) proposed temple, 1930. ENHANCED BY BILL CURTIS.

That a committee of three shall be selected, to outline the plans and specifications for the Temple (based upon the plans thus far received from various sources, as well as what may be received hereafter), before further excavation and construction work shall be undertaken. These plans to be drafted under the direction of the Twelve, and submitted to them for approval. And when so approved, to be submitted to a competent architect, for the purpose of obtaining sketches, blue prints, and estimations as to cost of construction, as well as specifications for material and equipment.[10]

The process of securing an architect fell to a re-constituted "Committee of Three." After interviewing several candidates, the committee felt inspired to select Norman Wilkinson of

Twelve" has been used interchangeably with "Quorum of Twelve Apostles," "Council of Twelve," and "Council of Apostles."

[10] Ibid., 74.

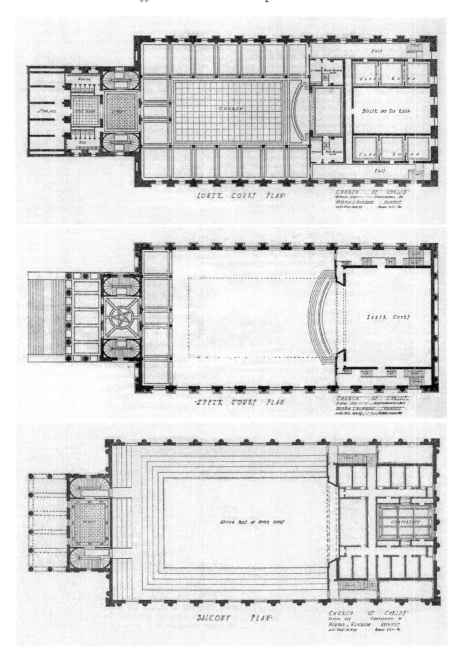

Wilkinson's architectural drawings of the Church of Christ (Temple Lot) proposed temple, 1930. Enhanced by Bill Curtis.

Kansas City, Missouri. The *Independence Examiner* announced the selection on April 16, 1930. Wilkinson was "instructed to follow closely the specifications indicated in the alleged divine instructions delivered to the church at a general conference two years ago."[11]

Four months later, on August 15, 1930, the *Independence Examiner* announced with a bold column heading: "Go Ahead with Temple." The article that followed quoted recently chosen architect Norman Wilkinson, who had responded to an interview request. He stated: "Architectural sketches will be done in about ten days." When asked about the probable cost of the proposed temple, Wilkinson stated: "the cost would be somewhere around a half million dollars." In the same article, Apostle Clarence L. Wheaton was quoted as saying:

> The work remaining to be done on the present excavation includes the taking out of another foot of earth in the main excavation and the excavation under the vestibule and portico.[12]

Wheaton also declared that:

> It is the intention and plan of the Church of Christ to continue with the building as soon as the working drawings are available.[13]

The Temple Fund balance at this time was $1285.00 and Wilkinson had been paid $250.00 for services rendered.[14]

The August 1, 1930, edition of *Zion's Advocate* pleaded with the church members everywhere to donate to the Temple Fund and to do so now as funds were desperately needed. The editorial urged: "Send in your contributions, be they ever so small, for it is now up to us to push the work forward or cause it to lag

---

[11] "Choose an Architect," *Independence Examiner*, April 16, 1930.

[12] "Go Ahead with Temple," *Independence Examiner*, August 15, 1930. An amount of $700,000 had been previously quoted.

[13] Ibid.

[14] "Financial Report of the General Church Office: March 15 to July 1 [1931]," *Zion's Advocate* 7, no. 12 (August 1, 1930): 126.

behind," and further commented that the steel and concrete in the trenches needed to be accomplished "this fall, but we *must have more money than we now have on hand*, for we are not going to contract debt with any man or men."[15] Meanwhile, on August 5, 1930, "the first load of rock for the trenches was hauled and dumped on the Temple Lot."[16]

As promised, Wilkinson proceeded to prepare his architectural drawings which were, in fact, prepared in less than ten days.[17] The *Kansas City Star* headlined and showcased, on the front page of their September 7, 1930, edition, the sketches of the "Extraordinary Temple the Church of Christ Has Begun to Build."[18]

With architectural drawings in hand, the Church of Christ published a special "Temple Number" as part of the November 1930 edition of *Zion's Advocate*. It had the same sketches that had appeared in local newspapers but also had reproductions of actual architectural drawings with dimensions and explanations. Also featured were photos of the two stones uncovered at the temple site in 1929. Numerous "temple oriented" articles also were included and, of course, a request for contributions to the Temple Fund was earnestly solicited, such as: "Are you one who will help in the erection of this building — the Temple of the Lord?"[19]

---

[15] Ibid., 127. Italics in original.

[16] "Proclamation," *Zion's Advocate* 7, no. 14 (September 1, 1930): 147.

[17] "Go Ahead with Temple," *Independence Examiner*, August 15, 1930.

[18] "The Outer Court of the Extraordinary Temple the Church of Christ Has Begun to Build with the Intention of Creating a Structure Which Will Defy the Ages," *Kansas City Star*, September 7, 1930, 1.

[19] Norman L. Wilkinson, "Description of Church of Christ Temple at Independence, Missouri," *Zion's Advocate* 7, no. 17 (November 1930): 169; "Who?," *Zion's Advocate* 7, no. 17 (November 1930): 178.

Efforts Continued: 1931–1933

OVERLAPPING THE NEED for money to get the Temple project restarted, was the reality that the general funds of the church were basically depleted. It was reported at the April 1931 conference of the church that during the past year $5,774 had been collected for the General Fund and $5,522 had been spent. The balance of the General Fund, at fiscal year-end, was a worrisome $252. The Temple Fund, it was reported, had receipted $2636 in donations during the year ending March 15, 1930. Expenditures had totaled $2248. The fiscal year-end balance of the Temple Fund was a troubling $388.[1]

By 1931 the economic situation in the United States was very serious. The onset of the "Great Depression," no doubt, had a major impact on the financial aspect of "getting back" to the Temple project. While the temple was very much on the minds of the members, there appeared to have been a shift in emphasis to the "Financial Law" of the church, the definition (and the collection) of "tithing," and preparing to live the "Law of Consecration" as revealed to Joseph Smith Jr. one hundred years previous.

To deal with the church debt issue, the Council of Apostles and General Bishopric had met August 10-15, 1930, in Independence (a year earlier) to discuss church finances.[2] The

[1] Arthur M. Smith, "Office Manager's Financial Report," *Zion's Advocate* 8, no. 9 (May 1, 1931): 68.

[2] Hiram E. Moler, William F. Anderson, Elmer E. Long, Arthur M. Smith, C. W. Morgan, Samuel Wood, Clarence L. Wheaton, of the Twelve; Alma O. Frisbey and John T. Ford, of the Bishops, "An Opinion on the Law of Tithing and Other Matters," *Zion's Advocate* 7, no. 14 (September 1, 1930): 148. Also see R. Jean

Church of Christ (Temple Lot) Apostle James E. Yates,
CHURCH OF CHRIST (TEMPLE LOT)

main emphasis of the letter to the members of the church was a call to "pay your tithing." The "Law of Tithing" was once again defined and its uses explained. Additionally, a "Proclamation" was issued "To the Saints and Friends of God Everywhere" requesting donations specifically for the construction of the temple.[3]

In preparing for the April 1931 conference, Apostle Bert C. Flint wrote the lead article in the April issue of *Zion's Advocate* under the heading: "Does a Material Temple Have Any Place in the Gospel?" The article began:

> Strange as it may seem among believers in the great Latter Day Restoration, who for nearly a century have been committed to the idea of a Zionic gathering and the building of a temple, on a spot dedicated by Joseph Smith and his associates, near the time of the

---

Addams, "The Church of Christ (Temple Lot) and the Law of Consecration," *John Whitmer Historical Association Journal* 28 (2008): 88-113.

[3] "Proclamation," *Zion's Advocate* 7, no. 14 (September 1, 1930): 147.

Rendering of the Church of Christ (Temple Lot) projected temple at Independence. Norman Wilkinson, architect, 1930. ENHANCED BY BILL CURTIS.

beginning of this work; the time has now come when an answer to the above question must be given, because the opposition to the idea comes from those among our own ranks.[4]

Flint then proceeded to defend the concept by referring to the purpose of the "tabernacle, or temple," and "His command to build (Exodus 25:12)." He then recited the scriptural history from Moses to Solomon and finally to the rebuilt temple in Jerusalem at the time of Jesus' ministry.[5]

On April 9, 1931, while the annual church conference was still in session, Apostle James E. Yates received a revelation which was immediately proclaimed to those members assembled. The revelation stated in part:

In answer to your prayers, I therefore give unto you these few instructions and exhortations.

Concerning the building of Mine House the Temple, be ye not fretted for the passing of time, nor yet dismayed, for all My preparations are not open to your minds.

---

[4] Bert C. Flint, "Does a Material Temple Have Any Place in the Gospel?," *Zion's Advocate* 8, no. 7 (April 1931): 51.

[5] Ibid., 51.

> Let the work upon the foundation proceed according to the present plans that have been drawn when the sum of five thousand dollars shall have been accumulated in the treasury. Then come before Me again in prayer for My further instructions.[6]

The April 10, 1931, issue of the *Independence Examiner*, in fact, carried the pronouncement of this revelation with the headline: "Temple 'Revelation' At the Church of Christ." In commenting on the revelation, the article noted that work on the proposed temple had been "lagging during the past year."[7] The need to acquire $5000 before the "work upon the foundation"[8] could proceed forced the church, more than ever before, to concentrate on finances. This action was necessary both for the general well-being of the church as well as for the temple project.

Coinciding with the Yates revelation, the April 1931 *Torch of Truth* featured a front-page story headed: "The Opening of the Temple Mines."[9] The article quickly posed the question: "Are you interested in helping build this sacred edifice, the Temple of the Lord?" The editor (Apostle James E. Yates) then proceeded to describe a gold mine investment opportunity of which he had been included as a partner with a faithful Church of Christ couple "Brother L. R. Williams and wife of Berkeley, Calif." The couple held the controlling interest in the mine. He explained that the assays showed the yield to be from between "six to ten dollars per ton." The balance of the article exhorted the reader to "contribute" so that the required machinery could be

[6] James E. Yates, "Revealment in Answer to Faith and Prayer of the Assembly," *Zion's Advocate* 8, no. 13 (July 1, 1931): 101.

[7] "Temple 'Revelation' at the Church of Christ: Purported Divine Direction Concerning Resumption of Work on the Temple," *Independence Examiner*, April 10, 1931.

[8] James E. Yates, "Revealment in Answer to Faith and Prayer of the Assembly," *Zion's Advocate* 8, no. 13 (July 1, 1931): 101; C. A. Gurwell, "The Sum of Five Thousand Dollars," *Zion's Advocate* 8, no. 17 (September 1, 1931): 131.

[9] James E. Yates, "The Opening of the Temple Mines," *Torch of Truth* 6, no. 7 (April 1931): 1-5.

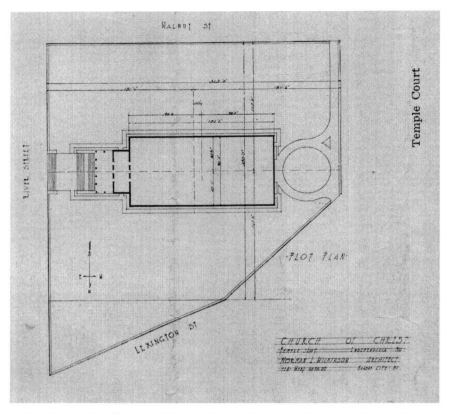

Site layout for Church of Christ (Temple Lot) temple prepared by architect Norman Wilkinson, 1930. ENHANCED BY BILL CURTIS.

installed. The initial amount needed was $1000. In concluding the article Yates stated:

> When you send what means you can spare for the operating of the Temple Mines, to obtain needed gold and silver for the Temple, if you wish merely that your funds be used for this development, and you desire your money returned when the returns from the mine make that possible, please so state, and your offering will be recorded in that way.
>
> Where the statement is not made that you wish your money back when it is possible to repay it from the products of the mine, it will be taken for granted that your offering is given without expecting the sum to be returned to you. In that case, the sum that you give,

together with such means as said sum can help to earn from the mine, will be turned over in due time to the Bishopric of the Church of Christ for the Temple, and will be used for the purchase of lands for the poor and for cooperative endeavor.[10]

This was not the first time, however, since the "sod was broken" that a speculative venture had been announced to the church with the anticipated profits to be dedicated toward building the Temple. In fact, the *Independence Examiner* reported on September 30, 1929: "Canadian Oil & Gas to Help Build Temple: Reported Big Find on MacGregor's [sic] Land."[11] The article then quoted Apostle Walter L. Gates who issued a statement for the Church of Christ: "We are expecting that this development will enable the church to make a big advance in the building on the temple this fall." The statement also noted that the location of the well and "the assurance that the oil was there" was reported to have been "revealed to Mr. and Mrs. Daniel MacGregor [sic] in 1914."[12] Nothing is readily known regarding the outcome of these ventures. It appears that no money, from either operation, was ever deposited into the Temple Fund.

Besides the indirect appeals for donations to the Temple Fund, direct solicitations continued through the balance of the year 1931. In September of that year, Bishop Thomas J. Jordan again requested the church to contribute to the building of the

---

[10] Ibid., 5.

[11] "Canadian Oil & Gas to Help Build Temple: Reported Big Find on MacGregor's [sic] Land at Oyen, Alberta, Canada, Hailed with Joy," *Independence Examiner*, September 30, 1929.

[12] Ibid. The subject of the Macgregor's involvement in Alberta, Canada, oil ventures had been a subject of significant interest within the RLDS Church in 1923. See C. Edward Miller, Letter to First Presidency and Presiding Bishopric, May 18, 1923, typed original and typescript, Miscellaneous Letters, P13, f1522, Israel A. Smith, Letter to Frederick M. Smith, June 2, 1923, typed original and typescript, Miscellaneous Letters, P13, f1531, and C. Edward Miller, Letter to Daniel Macgregor, July 5, 1923, typed original and typescript, Miscellaneous Letters, P13, f1540, Community of Christ Archives-Library, Independence, Missouri.

temple in an article titled simply: "Build the Temple."[13] In the same issue, Apostle James E. Yates published a poem (with a chorus) "written and adapted to the song: *The Church in the Wildwood*. The first verse and chorus exclaimed:

THE PLACE OF THE TEMPLE
There's a spot God hath chosen for the Temple
No lovelier place ever found,
T'is the word of Christ our Example,
By his word this is holy ground.

Chorus
O Come, come, come, come,
Come to the place of the Temple,
O, come to the Courts of the Lord,
No place that man selecteth
Can compare with the choice of his word.[14]

At the April 1932 conference of the Church of Christ, it was reported that the total amount of the funds collected for the Temple Fund for the fiscal year ended March 15, 1932 was $1499 and that expenditures were $125. This left a balance available of $1324.[15] Reflecting internal discouragement and the reality of the Great Depression, the April 1933 conference report for the Temple Fund showed only $587 in contributions. Expenditures were $1206, which left an on-hand balance of $702.[16]

At the conference of 1933, a document titled: "Recommendations of the Twelve Relative to Resuming Work on the Temple," was voted upon and adopted. It read:

---

[13] "Build the Temple," *Zion's Advocate* 8, no. 17 (September 1, 1931): 131.

[14] James E. Yates, "The Place of the Temple," *Zion's Advocate* 8, no. 17 (September 1, 1931): 133. As noted, only the first of four verses is shown above. Also, the chorus following verse four is different than that shown above.

[15] "General Assembly Minutes [1932]," *Zion's Advocate* 9, no. 5 (May 1932): 77.

[16] "General Assembly of the Church of Christ, 1933," *Zion's Advocate* 10, no. 4 (April 1933): 63.

Be it Resolved: That this Assembly encourage[s] the resuming of work on the Temple at the earliest possible moment, as follows:

First: That we take advantage of the offer of Brother E[lmer] E. Long with regard to quarrying rock on his place for concrete construction work on the Temple, with such voluntary labor as can be obtained.

Second: That we encourage the cutting and sawing of timbers on the land in South Missouri, offered by Brother Rathbone for cribbing the trenches and excavation, and the building of forms for the foundation of the Temple.

Third: That as soon as timbers can be delivered upon the ground, excavation work shall be started in harmony with the working plans approved by this 1933 General Assembly.

Fourth: That we make a consistent and studious effort to raise the sum of $5,000.00, as indicated in the manifestation of Apostle James E. Yates, before actual construction work, in the way of steel and concrete construction, shall be undertaken.

Fifth: That in order to facilitate the work, and place the responsibility of carrying into effect these provisions, that the Plans Committee be authorized to take oversight of this work and devise ways and means to resume work as herein provided.[17]

Elder Thomas J. Jordan announced at the April 12, 1933, session of the conference his divine communication and urged the church to prepare to resume work on the temple. Jordan also told of "a series of visions in which he said he saw a long procession of men with various kinds of implements in their hands, walk toward the present excavation for the Temple and begin work in laying the foundation; a phase of the work that never yet has been done or even started."[18]

This pronouncement, combined with the action of the church regarding the necessity of resuming the "work on the great temple of granite," spurred the church forward toward

[17] Clarence L. Wheaton (secretary of the Twelve), "Recommendations from the Twelve Relative to Resuming Work on the Temple," *Zion's Advocate* 10, no. 4 (April 1933): 52.

[18] "Says God Urges Work on Temple: Elder T[homas] J. Jordan Reports Divine Communication to Church of Christ Conference," *Independence Examiner*, April 13, 1933, 1.

Church of Christ (Temple Lot) excavation for temple, ca 1929-1930, COMMUNITY
OF CHRIST LIBRARY-ARCHIVES

finishing the foundation for the temple.[19] The May 1933 *Zion's Advocate* added a two-page cover to the standard edition of the paper. The cover featured, first, a photographic reproduction of a painting of the Savior with out-stretched arms and, second, a photographic reproduction of the architect's rendering of the completed temple.[20]

Obviously, the push was to "get back to work" on the temple project and to generate the necessary funds to meet the $5000 "minimum" established by the Yates' revelation of 1931. The headline on the front page of the May 1933 issue of *Zion's Advocate* (behind the two-page special cover) proclaimed: "It Is Time to Go to Work."[21] The story emphasized that part of the "Fifth Message" which had not been previously given much copy

[19] Ibid.

[20] *Zion's Advocate* 10, no. 5 (May 1933): cover.

[21] "It Is Time to Go to Work," *Zion's Advocate* 10, no. 5 (May 1933): 67.

(but which was certainly on the collective mind of the church), i.e., the required completion date for the temple of 1936. The church was strongly urged to "Rise Up and Build."[22]

The General Assembly in April 1933 also enacted the establishment of the "Storehouse Committee." The committee was to be composed of seven men. They were to be responsible for the finances of the church and a general storehouse. The resolution stated that the committee:

> Shall be intrusted [sic] to gather materials and supplies of every kind, including money and properties. These supplies to be the necessary material for the actual construction of the Temple, together with all other supplies of food, clothing, and the general need of: (a) Those who labor on the Temple, and their dependents[;] (b) Missionaries and their families who devote all their time to the work[;] (c) The poor and needy. Provided that all material and means of every sort belonging strictly to the Temple shall be kept separate from and under the head of Temple property.[23]

One of the ideas generated to raise funds for the temple project was a "Temple Bank." The bank was made of aluminum and measured about 3 × 6 inches in size and looked like the proposed temple as drawn by the Plans Committee and the architect. The price was $1.00. It was stated in an article describing the offering that "one of these banks should be in every home and church. They will serve as a constant reminder of the great task and commission that has been given to the members of the Church of Christ."[24]

As scheduled, the "Committee of Seven" convened in Independence on July 27, 1933. The July 26, 1933, edition of the *Independence Examiner*, which announced the arrival of the committee members, commented that the "chief purpose of the council will be to initiate plans for the collection and storing

---

[22] Ibid., 67.

[23] Walter L. Gates, "Committee of Seven to Meet: Time Set from July 27 to August 3, 1933," *Zion's Advocate* 10, no. 6 (June 1933): 85.

[24] "Temple Bank," *Zion's Advocate* 10, no. 6 (June 1933): 86.

of material to be used in the construction of the proposed temple."[25] On the following day (July 27) the *Independence Examiner* carried a headline which announced: "Excavators Busy on Temple Site." The article stated that "construction work on the proposed temple of the Church of Christ, on the Temple Lot, has been resumed after two or more years of inactivity."[26]

The July 1933 edition of *Zion's Advocate* featured a photograph of four men and two horses. The caption read: "The Temple of the Lord in Zion — Actual Work on the Excavation Begins in Earnest."[27] In a lengthy article in the August 1933 edition of the same periodical, Apostle Clarence L. Wheaton reported on the purchase of horses and a scraper and that progress was underway toward completing the excavation for the temple. In an interesting plea to the farmers of the church Wheaton urged:

> If several of you farmers in the church, that are interested in the building of the Temple, would get your heads together and see what you can donate to the Temple work in the way of hay, corn, and oats. Baled hay, of course, would be best, but loose hay will be accepted, and a way provided to transport it here. Let us hear from you as early as convenient.[28]

As a prelude to the events of the next three years, Apostle James E. Yates, editor of the independent newspaper the *Torch of Truth*, stated in the September 25, 1933 issue: "When this Temple so long dreamed of is built at the sacred place, it will be when all divisions of the Church of the Restoration develope

---

[25] "Church of Christ Committee Meets: To Expedite Building of Temple by Gifts of Materials and Labor the Purpose of Five Days Session," *Independence Examiner*, July 26, 1933.

[26] "Ready to Donate Work for Temple," *Independence Examiner*, July 27, 1933.

[27] Walter L. Gates, "The Temple of the Lord in Zion: Actual Work Begins in Earnest," *Zion's Advocate* 10, no. 7 (August 1933): 93-4.

[28] Clarence L. Wheaton, "Work on Temple Encouraging," *Zion's Advocate* 10, no. 8 (August 1933): 109-10.

[sic] enough of real Christianity... to join hands in the building of this Temple."[29]

The December 1933 publication of *Zion's Advocate* featured a large photo of the temple excavation which had been dug to the required depth of nine feet and eleven inches. The photo depicted nine individuals posed on the floor of the excavation (see page 91). The caption accompanying the photo noted that "four of the foundation caissons have been sunk to the solid rock and can now be filled with the concrete and steel."[30] The article following the photo was another plea to the members of the church for immediate financial aid to fund the cost of the necessary concrete and steel. While no mention was made of the $5000 minimum balance (the Yates revelation) needed in the Temple Fund before any material work on the temple could begin, the final comment in the article proclaimed: "Therefore, let the Temple of the Lord be built."[31]

[29] James E. Yates, "The Building of the Temple," *Torch of Truth* 8, no. 6 (September 25, 1933): 1. Chronologically this issue should be Volume 8 (as shown). However, the masthead of this issue states that it is Volume 5. Photocopy of paper in author's possession.

[30] "The Divine Edifice: Ready for Concrete and Steel," *Zion's Advocate* 10, no. 12 (December 1933): 133.

[31] Ibid., 134.

Efforts Continued: 1934–1935

T HE COVER PAGE of the first issue of *Zion's Advocate* for the year 1934 published a poem "A Prayer for the Temple."[1] The call to "go forward" in spite of the lingering "Depression" and their struggles to raise funds was still very much alive.

During the April 1934 conference of the church, the matter of physically getting back to work on the temple was apparently, however, not officially discussed. The only matters presented that related to the temple were (1) a motion to invite other factions to appoint two members each, as an advisory committee to act in conjunction with the Building Committee. (This motion was "laid upon the table," not because the spirit and intent were not appreciated, but because it was thought to be premature")[2] and (2) a motion that stated: "That from now on the Plans' Committee and the Building Committee [to] be separate committees." (This motion carried.)[3]

Perhaps an underlying reason why nothing was specifically discussed relative to the temple project was that the auditing committee was not ready to report the financial situation of the church, including the Temple Fund. The committee asked the assembly if they could have their report published in the next edition of *Zion's Advocate*. This request was apparently granted

---

[1] "A Prayer for the Temple," *Zion's Advocate* 11, no. 1 (January 1934): 1. No name of the poet/author is given.

[2] "General Assembly for 1934," *Zion's Advocate* 11, no. 2 (April 1934): 14.

[3] Ibid., 13.

Church of Christ (Temple Lot) meetinghouse and excavation site for temple, late 1930s or early 1940s, WILFORD C. WOOD FOUNDATION

although the minutes of the conference do not indicate one way or the other.[4]

Throughout the fiscal year, April 1, 1933 – March 31, 1934, the church was able to raise only $305 for the Temple Fund, hardly enough for the cement and steelwork needed. With the carryover funds from the previous year, less the expenditures incurred during the course of the past fiscal year, the balance of the Temple Fund on March 31, 1934, was only $152.[5] Total church membership (as of March 1934) stood at 1825, an increase of about 80 over the previous year.[6]

During the summer of 1934, Apostle William F. Anderson authored an urgent appeal to the church titled: "Let Us Go Forward." He remarked:

> The Temple has not been built, not because God has failed, but because the people of His choice have refused to do as asked, choosing rather to listen to the promptings of an opposite force.

[4] Ibid., 13-4.

[5] Ibid., 14. (Financial Report).

[6] Ibid., 14.

Anderson then reminded the church that "God directed the building of a Temple," then pleaded:

> We have tarried too long. Let us arise and build, fearing nothing...We need God; we need a Zion; we need the Temple, or God would never have said to build it.[7]

Following Anderson's appeal, the Temple Building Committee published a "Notice" in the same issue of *Zion's Advocate*. It stated that they (the committee) will "dig the trenches to the rock, as directed." Again an appeal for help, equipment, food, and money was made to the membership of the church.[8]

Apparently, some work was done on the excavation in the late summer of 1934. A report in the October 1934 *Zion's Advocate* noted:

> Rains have interrupted the work on the excavation for the temple, but we are thankful for the rain, and the workers are going to quarry rock on Brother Long's place, we were told, while they are waiting for the soil to dry. The rock is going to be needed, so no time is lost.[9]

That same month (October 1934), Elder Thomas B. Nerren, Superintendent of Temple Construction, reported a revelation he had received while asleep "in his room at the Home for Temple Construction." The crux of the revelation stated:

> Now, if you, My people, will hearken and go forward as I commanded, I will remove the barriers that stand in the way and have hindered My work, both as to building of My Temple, and the preaching of My Gospel.[10]

---

[7] William F. Anderson, "Let Us Go Forward," *Zion's Advocate* 11, no. 6 (August 1934): 43.

[8] "Notice from the Building Committee," *Zion's Advocate* 11, no. 6 (August 1934): 43.

[9] "Independence," *Zion's Advocate* 11, no. 8 (October 1934): 61.

[10] Thomas B. Nerren, "Revelation Given to T[homas] B. Nerren, Superintendent of Temple Construction," October 1934, Independence, Missouri. This is a single sheet or broadside. Photocopy in possession of the author. Nerren had returned to activity in the Church of Christ and his 1929 "silencing" had been, obviously, lifted.

Ethel Holcomb writing for *Zion's Advocate* in its March 1935 edition, urged the members of the Church of Christ to:

> At all times keep the building of the temple in our minds and help all we can by work, donations of money, clothes, or anything that can be used in the building, or by the workers who are engaged upon it. It should be our hope, aim and ambition to build it in the allotted time, so that the Lord will not have to raise up another people to build his house. He has given us over one hundred years for the purpose and so far the work has not been accomplished.[11]

The *Independence Examiner* announced on April 5, 1935, before the commencement of the annual conference, that it "is expected that there will be much discussion and perhaps some action, during the business session of the general assembly of the Church of Christ, on the Temple Lot, which will open its annual session Saturday morning here, in regard to their proposed temple." The article further reported:

> Great quantities of timber have been prepared for use in this temple, at Atherton and at Cross Timbers, Mo., especially at the latter place and that a strong disposition exists on the part of officials and other members to take up the work again.[12]

Six days later, while the church conference was still in session, the *Independence Examiner* reported that "a special committee composed of Apostles E[lmer] E. Long, James E. Yates, and Clarence L. Wheaton had been appointed to consider "resuming work on the building of the temple." The *Examiner* also commented that the committee was "ready to report to the general assembly" that they favored "the continuance of the preparation of building materials to be used in the temple, as has been going on during the past year." The article also

---

[11] Ethel Holcomb, "Help Build the Temple," *Zion's Advocate* 12, no. 3 (March 1935): 30.

[12] "May Resume Work on Temple Here: General Assembly of Church of Christ on Temple Lot, Opening Saturday, Will Discuss the Project," *Independence Examiner*, April 5, 1935, 1.

mentioned that they "would recommend that a referendum be
held on a proposition to invite members of other Mormon sects
to co-operate, as individuals, with the Church of Christ, in the
building of the Temple."[13]

Following the conference, Apostle E[lmer] E. Long
presented a document "urging speed with the work of building
the temple." Soon thereafter the Temple Building Committee
reported to the church:

> On the whole, the outlook is encouraging, but we need co-operation
> and help. We need money to buy cement and steel. The Lord has told
> us that this house is to be built by 'the tithing of my people,' and by
> 'sacrifice.' No debt is to be incurred. We must pay as we go so as to
> 'owe no man anything.'[14]

At the April 1935 conference, Bishop Thomas J. Jordan called
for a "detailed, itemized account from the building committee of
the expenditure of the Temple funds."[15] Two months later, the
Building Committee, as requested, issued a "Quarterly Report"
to the Council of Twelve. The first item discussed "was to finish
[the] sawing of logs. This we did…and the lumber was stacked
on the Temple Lot, 30,000 [board] feet." Also noted by the
committee was that "the tool house and shop at the west end
of the lot is [sic] finished…so that tools and other equipment
could be safely cared for." Furthermore, Apostle Elmer E. Long,
chairman, indicated that there was "sufficient crushed rock and
sand on the ground to make the contemplated start, an[d] as

---

[13] "Two Bishops By Divine Guidance," *Independence Examiner*, April 11, 1935, 1.

[14] Elmer E. Long, Charles E. Derry, Thomas B. Nerran, John E. Bozarth, and I. C.
Pierce, "From the Building Committee, dated May 8, 1935," *Zion's Advocate* 11, no.
6 (June 1935): 71. See R. Jean Addams, "The Church of Christ (Temple Lot) and
the Law of Consecration," *John Whitmer Historical Association Journal*, (2008), vol.
28, 105-10.

[15] "General Assembly of Church of Christ, Fifth Day, Wednesday, April 10, Afternoon
Session," *Zion's Advocate* 11, no. 5 (May 1935): Supplement, 5.

soon as the money is on hand to buy the steel we expect to put the steel in place."[16]

Finally, the committee suggested that the matter of housing and feeding the workers was too expensive (referring to the past policy). The recommendation stated:

> It appears to us that it would be cheaper to hire as needed and at the same time employ such donated [labor, hand-written in the margin] as may be offered by those who are self sustaining.

The balance in the Temple Fund as of June 28, 1935 was $3.86.[17]

The Building Committee attached five resolutions to their report. Among them, "Resolution #4" proclaimed:

> That we may put to test, God's promise made to this Church, in a Revelation given to it in 1930 [1931] through Apostle James E. Yates-- 'when the sum of $5000 shall have been accumulated in the treasury come before me again in prayer for my further instructions,' —we do now pledge ourselves and our united efforts to the task of 'accumulating this $5000.'[18]

In another effort to stimulate interest and push the temple project forward, the 1870 "Temple Dream" of Elder George D. Cole was reprinted in *Zion's Advocate* in the fall of 1935.[19]

---

[16] Quarterly Report of the Building Committee, addressed: "To the Quorum of the Twelve, June 28, 1935." This is a two-page single spaced typed report signed by "E[lmer] E. Long, Chairman Committee and Cha[rles] E. Derry, Secretary Committee." Additionally a two-page typed list of suggested "resolutions," is attached. The report is also accompanied by a cover letter addressed to "Brother [Clarence L.] Wheaton" and signed by Elmer E. Long. Photocopy in possession of the author.

[17] Ibid., Report, 2.

[18] Ibid., Suggested Resolutions, 2.

[19] George D. Cole, "Temple Dream," *Zion's Advocate* 12, no. 10 (October 1935): 113-14. Rpt of article from the *Evening and Morning Star*, March 1916 and *Zion's Advocate*, November 1926. Cole relates that the dream occurred "not long after I had joined the church." Cole was baptized on April 9, 1870.

Outside pressures continued to mount for the Church of Christ in their quest to build the temple. Elder Thomas B. Nerren, in a letter written to Apostle Arthur M. Smith on December 6, 1935, reported the story of a recent meeting of the Independence school board. In quoting Alva Wheaton he remarked that only one vote was lacking to "condemn the Temple Lot (as a public nuisance). They [the school board] wanted to build a new school on it."[20]

Nerren also commented in his letter that he had personally sent out letters (1935), at his own expense, "asking for money for steel or concrete or tile...in building the Temple. These brought many dollars into the office."[21] Obviously, the matter of generating enough money into the Temple Fund (to reach the $5000) for the needed "steel and cement," continued to be a major frustration to the Building Committee and to the church.

[20] Thomas B. Nerren, Letter to Arthur M. Smith, December 6, 1935. This is hand-written six-page letter. Photocopy in possession of the author. Also see, Paul E. Reimann, "A Generous gift from the First Presidency in 1950 for Education at Independence, Missouri," MS 7168, Church History Library, Salt Lake City, Utah. The gift was a direct response by the LDS Church to the potential process of eminent domain by the City of Independence, Missouri, wherein the City of Independence could take possession of the vacant land (purchased by the LDS Church in 1904 and part of the 63¼ acres) to build a new high school. The mayor of Independence and the city's school board president traveled to Salt Lake City in 1950 to discuss the matter with LDS Church President George A. Smith. A $25,000 donation was given to the city, by the LDS Church, toward another site/high school. The amount was, ironically, the same amount that the LDS Church originally paid for the 26 acre tract of land in 1904.

[21] Thomas B. Nerren, Letter to Arthur M. Smith, December 6, 1935. This is hand-written six-page letter. Photocopy in possession of the author.

Efforts Continued: 1936–1942

A S THE YEAR 1936 began, members of the Church of Christ were well aware that the seven year time-frame originally provided for in Otto Fetting's "Fifth Message" was about to expire. Undaunted, the church pushed forward. In January 1936, the general office manager, Bishop James R. McClain, reiterated the church policies of "no debt" and "specific application." The Bishop explained that if a member donated to the Temple Fund and specifically designated the donation to be for the "steel fund" it would be "used for nothing else" and "will not be used even to buy food or other supplies for the workers."[1]

As the April 1936 conference time drew near, the *Independence Examiner* speculated that:

> It is probable that much of the business of its [the Church of Christ] coming general conference will have to do with the resumption of construction work on the proposed temple, which was started several years ago, but on which little was done during "the depression" except to assemble some building material.[2]

However, rather than urging the saints to again renew their efforts towards building the temple as had been anticipated in the press, a major proposition was presented to the assembled conference. It was the most significant resolution and vote the church had taken on any matter in ten years. The purpose of this

---

[1] James R. McClain, "New Years Greeting: From the General Office Manager," *Zion's Advocate* 13, no. 1 (January 1936): 2.

[2] "Another Conference Too: Church of Christ on Temple Lot Will Also Open Its Meetings Monday," *Independence Examiner*, April 4, 1936, 1.

proposal was the repudiation of the so-called "Fetting Messages." Many in the church had been expressing their feelings in this regard for the past three or four years. Their concerns had been repeatedly tabled or set aside in previous years. However, on April 10, 1936, a specific motion was offered and seconded as follows:

> Whereas, it is the position of the Church of Christ that 'purported revealments from God must stand on their own merits as they may be demonstrated by the arbitraments of time;' And Whereas, the passing of time and events have proven that the error contained in the messages given by the late Otto Fetting show them to be unreliable as being the word of the Lord; And Whereas, even the partial and qualified approval with reservations which the church gave to said purported revelations in the year 1930 has proven to be an impediment to righteousness in the church and not a blessing,
>
> Therefore, and in the interest of spiritual progress for the church, be it hereby declared that we consider ourselves justly absolved from any supposed allegiance to those messages as being the work of God.
>
> Our present temple plans are not based wholly upon said messages, and not at all except where they were not out of agreement with revelations concerning the temple as given through the prophet, Joseph;
>
> And our continued work of building the temple shall not conform to any specifications supposed to have been given by John the Baptist to Otto Fetting merely because said specifications might appear in some of those unreliable messages.[3]

Much discussion, both pro and con, followed the introduction of this motion until it was time to adjourn for the day. The following morning the discussion of the matter before the conference continued. At length a vote on the motion was called and carried: 23 for and 8 against.[4]

Immediately following the vote to repudiate the Fetting "Messages," Apostle Elmer E. Long requested the floor of the

---

[3] "Minutes of the General Ministers' Conference of the Church of Christ," *Zion's Advocate* 13, no. 5 (May 1936): 53.

[4] Ibid., 54.

conference as a personal privilege and offered his resignation as follows:

> Inasmuch as you have adopted the resolution repudiating the messages pertaining to the building of the temple and other matters of Church policy, thereby vitiating my calling as an apostle, I hereby present my resignation as a representative of the Church of Christ.[5]

Long's decision was reluctantly accepted by those assembled.

On Monday afternoon, April 13, a new motion was offered and carried. It read:

> That with [the] exception of such work as may be necessary to protect that which has been done[;] the work on the temple shall be continued after the sum of at least five thousand dollars ($5000) has been accumulated in the temple fund treasury.[6]

The next day one of the items of business presented to the assembly was a report on the Temple Fund. The fund activity showed receipts for the past year of $1,016, expenses of $1,185, and a bank balance of $169.[7]

Two days later the *Independence Examiner* reported:

> Although the general conference of the Church of Christ, Temple Lot, Independence, has lost hope of being able to carry on rapidly the work of building its temple, it appointed a temple building committee, Tuesday, to function during the ensuing year.
>
> The main duty of this committee, for the present, at least, would be to take care of some building materials that have been assembled on the grounds, and to do some emergency work to prevent deterioration of the work already done, mostly excavation.
>
> Elaborate plans for the temple based on specifications furnished by the late Otto Fetting on the strength of alleged divine communications, have been in the hands of such a committee several years, but little has

---

[5] Ibid., 55.

[6] Ibid., 54.

[7] Ibid., 56.

RLDS Church Auditorium under construction, COMMUNITY OF
CHRIST LIBRARY-ARCHIVES

been done except make the excavation, and assemble some lumber
intended to be used in making forms for concrete.[8]

Meanwhile on May 5, 1936, Apostle Clarence L. Wheaton,
in a letter addressed to: "All Members of the Church of Christ
(Temple Lot) in the Northwestern States Mission," and
specifically to the attention of Elder Robert T. Newby, pointed
out another measure adopted by the Minister's Conference the
previous month.[9] The matter Wheaton referred to was the re-
establishment of a "committee on working harmony between
the Church of Christ and other divisions of the restoration."
He pointed out that there had already been contacts made with
the other major divisions of the Restoration. Wheaton then
discussed the disappointment and frustration in the building of
the temple. He stressed the effects of Satan in leading "many

[8] "A Temple Building Committee is Named: Main Duty of Church of Christ Group
Will Be to Assemble Materials on Grounds," *Independence Examiner*, April 15, 1936,
3.

[9] Clarence L. Wheaton, Letter to "All Members of the Church of Christ (Temple Lot)
in the Northwestern States Mission," May 5, 1936, 2. This is a six-page single spaced
typewritten letter, postmarked Sagle, Idaho. Photocopy in possession of the author.

of our most valiant" members of the ministry into "spiritual destruction."[10]

Finally, Wheaton turned this multi-page letter into a discourse dealing with failure to complete the temple in seven years. He wrote: "In spite of the sacrifices, which for our small group have been collossal [sic], the promises contained therein [the "Messages"] have proven to be false and a delusion." He then added: "Nothing fundamental to the Restoration of 1830 is lost by the repudiation of them."[11]

As provided for in church rules, all motions approved at the annual conference were to be published and mailed out to all members of the church in the form of a referendum for a vote. The September 1936 *Zion's Advocate* reported the tabulation of the voting on those motions approved at the April 1936 conference of the church.[12] The motion to repudiate the "Fetting Messages" was known as "Bill No. 10." The vote was 313 to 99 to repudiate. The motion regarding the resumption of the temple construction and the necessity of accumulating $5000 in the Temple Fund was known as "Bill No. 15." It also carried by a vote of 302 to 58. Additionally, "Bill No. 35" which provided that all monies in the Temple Fund be turned over to the Bishopric was, overwhelmingly, carried by a vote of 381 to 14.[13]

Meanwhile, the RLDS Church struggled with its own financial problems during the 1930s, especially regarding the

---

[10] Ibid., 3.

[11] Ibid., 5.

[12] "The People's Conference: 1936 Result of the Referendum Vote," *Zion's Advocate* 13, no. 9 (September 1936): 101-03. The usual procedure was to include the Referendum(s) as a separate part or section of the May issue of *Zion's Advocate*. The section would have its own heading: "Supplement." The Referendum(s) would be printed on separate pages with a "tear-out" ballot that the member was instructed to mail in to church headquarters in Independence, Missouri. Ballots had to be receipted before a specified deadline to be accepted. Thereafter, the ballots would be tabulated by a designated committee and reported some months later in a subsequent issue of *Zion's Advocate*.

[13] Ibid., 102.

construction of the Auditorium. During this time period the rhetoric between these two neighbors of the Restoration quieted down. On July 3, 1936, RLDS Church Historian Samuel A. Burgess responded to a letter written to the church by a Sister Mabel Burns. The essence of Burns' questions had to do with the Church of Christ's efforts to build their temple. Burgess indicated that the Church of Christ had "excavated several years ago a hole for the basement and ran some holes down to rock for the pouring of the lower pillars. This was cleaned out again last year [1935]." He provided additional detail and then closed with this statement:

> They are making [an] approach to all of the other factions, including the Utah faction and ours, for a group effort cooperative, to build this temple that they plan. How far they will succeed in erecting it is not yet apparent.[14]

In early May 1936, the LDS Church in Salt Lake City, Utah, was contacted by officers of the Church of Christ regarding the proposed cooperative effort. On May 8, 1936, Elder David O. McKay, a member of the LDS Church's Quorum of Twelve Apostles, recorded in his diary: "Attended to current duties including writing a reply to a committee of the Church of Christ, Independence, Missouri, inviting our church to join in building a temple in Jackson County. We courteously refused."[15]

Without the $5000 in the Temple Fund and with rejections or "no response" from other factions of the Restoration, the

---

[14] Samuel A. Burgess, Letter to Mabel Burns, July 3, 1936, Miscellaneous Samuel A. Burgess Correspondence Collection, Community of Christ Library-Archives, Independence, Missouri. Mabel Burns was a member of the Church of Christ living in Detroit, Michigan. It is noteworthy that she was writing the RLDS Church for specific information.

[15] David O. McKay, Diary, entry dated May 8, 1936, transcribed, Gregory A. Prince Papers, Accn 1334, Special Collections, Marriott Library, University of Utah, Salt Lake City, Utah. Prince's donated materials were originally obtained in preparation for the recently published *David O. McKay and The Rise of Modern Mormonism* by Gregory A. Prince and Wm. Robert Wright (University of Utah Press: Salt Lake City, Utah, 2005).

temple project was in serious jeopardy. These frustrations carried over to the next church conference.

In January 1937, Apostle Leon A. Gould, in a message to the church, asked rhetorically: "When will we build the Temple [?]" and answered: "When we go about it in the right way." He quoted a revelation received by Joseph Smith Jr. in September 1832. Here the Lord instructs the prophet regarding "the city New Jerusalem: which city shall be built, beginning at the Temple Lot...that the city New Jerusalem shall be built by the gathering of the Saints, beginning at this place, even the place of the temple, which temple shall be reared in this generation." (RLDS D&C 83:1-2.b. and LDS D&C 84:1-5). Gould then continued:

> Twice in the foregoing quotation the declaration is made that the building of the New Jerusalem is to begin at the Temple Lot, the place of the Temple. The building of the one is to [be] a concomitant of the building of the other. If we are able to determine the laws to govern in the building of Zion, or the New Jerusalem, we may safely conclude that the same laws put in operation will dispel the fog, clear the atmosphere, and open the way for a successful undertaking relative to the building of the Temple.

Gould then concluded by stating what he thought those laws referred to were, specifically: "(1) A Complete Consecration!; (2) A Storehouse and a Common Fund; and (3) An Equitable Distribution Through the Storehouse."[16]

At the April church conference of 1937, it was proposed that the committee "on Working Harmony" be abolished, no doubt due to the above mentioned failure to secure help from the other divisions of the Restoration.[17] The matter was much discussed on the fourth day of the conference and then revisited the following day. Again, after considerable discussion,

---

[16] Leon A. Gould, "When Will We Build the Temple [?]," *Zion's Advocate* 14, no. 1 (January 1937): 152-55.

[17] "Minutes of the General Minister's Conference of the Church of Christ 1937," *Zion's Advocate* 14, no. 5 (May 1937): 197.

the matter was "tabled." Two days later, a substitute resolution was presented. It read:

> Whereas there has been so much contention over the Working Harmony movement and the committee;
>
> And whereas we have now spent two days on this matter and are just where we were when we started;
>
> Therefore, be it resolved that this body in conference assembled, by their vote ask this committee to resign, and that contact with the other groups of the Restoration be made through the ministry of the Church of Christ (Temple Lot) which is a continuation of the church restored April 6, 1830.[18]

No doubt the reason for the three days of discussion and disagreement had to do with the details of the report presented at the conference and the continued commentary, both written and oral, that preceded the ballot voting by the church members on the "Referendum — Bills for 1937."[19]

On April 10, 1937, the *Independence Examiner* reported that:

> The business session [of the Church of Christ] Friday afternoon [April 9] was occupied mainly in considering the matter of a 'working agreement' with other factions of Mormonism. This position originated in the general conference a year or two ago.

The reporter then speculated:

> Much of the time of the session next week will be devoted to a consideration of the project of building the proposed temple, for which the excavations were made and some building material...assembled[,] but little actual construction work done for the past two years.[20]

---

[18] Ibid., 200.

[19] Ibid., Supplement.

[20] "Will Consider the Building of Temple: Church of Christ Expects to Discuss Project Next Week — Talk of Agreement with Other Sects," *Independence Examiner*, April 10, 1937, 1.

In this statement the reporter erred. In fact, on April 13, 1937, the bishops of the church presented a report to the conference relative to the temple project that stated, in part:

> In view of the fact that the lumber on the Temple Lot is deteriorating very fast, the one inch stuff especially, that it be sold for cash, and placed in the temple fund, with which other material may be purchased when needed, if not otherwise provided for by the conference: 'that the office manager, Brother [James R.] McClain, and A[lva] S. Wheaton be authorized to sell the lumber.' This action was concurred in by four bishops present. This to also include the cement that was left on hand by the Building committee.[21]

Finally, the "Report of the Temple Plans Committee" was read to the assembly and subsequently printed in the May 1937 issue of *Zion's Advocate*. It stated:

> The Temple Plans Committee respectfully reports that, as known to the Church, there has been no construction work on the Temple during the year, and for that reason there was no occasion for any action by the Plans Committee.
>
> When the time arrives that there shall be sufficient means in the treasury to place the necessary cement and steel in the foundation of the Temple, and to bring the basement of the structure to the top of the excavation, we as your Plans Committee stand ready to do our humble part in coordinating the specifications of the Plans as they are drafted with the progress of the work of construction.
>
> Let not our hearts lose faith; the Temple will be erected in this place, and according to the word of the Lord which has been given.[22]

The balance in the Temple Fund as of March 15, 1937, and reported to the conference was $205. The church membership stood at 2007.[23]

---

[21] "Minutes of the General Minister's Conference of the Church of Christ 1937," *Zion's Advocate* 14, no. 5, (May 1937): 201.

[22] Ibid., 204.

[23] Ibid.

The June issue of *Zion's Advocate* carried thirteen pages of commentary from four church apostles,[24] concluding with Clarence L. Wheaton's article: "Shall the Committee on Working Harmony Be Abolished?" the subject matter of which he had previously preached as a sermon on the Temple Lot on Sunday evening, May 9, 1937.[25] Wheaton discussed many of the points that had been argued over at the previous conference. He focused his concern, however, on the ownership of the temple when it was completed provided that other branches of the Restoration facilitated in its construction. He stated:

> If the hearts of other organic bodies within the faith of the Latter Day Restoration shall be moved upon to join in erecting the Temple of the Lord, should we arrogantly refuse that cooperation? We believe that such a demonstration of faith in the promises of God upon their part, would entitle them to share in the legal and possessive ownership of the Temple when it is finished. Furthermore, they should have [a] guarantee beforehand, that such bonifide [sic] share of title will be faithfully issued when the structure is finished and ready to be dedicated. Why not? If they conform to the requirement of the true faith in Christ, and in accord with His law?[26]

As stated above, virtually the entire edition of the June 1937 *Zion's Advocate*, issued six weeks after the conclusion of the conference, was devoted to articles, both pro and con, on whether or not to abolish the "Committee on Working Harmony." The main thrust behind the effort to abolish this committee had to do with the temple project and how and why the Church of

---

[24] Bert C. Flint, Arthur M. Smith, James E. Yates, and Clarence L. Wheaton, "Discussion of Bills Nos. 10, 11, 29," *Zion's Advocate* 14, no. 6 (June 1937): 211-23. Each apostle's article was sub-titled: Flint, "Concerning the Committee on Working Harmony;" Smith, "Why I Am Not in Favor of the Committee on Working Harmony;" Yates, "Charity, Kindness, and 'Working Harmony;'" and Wheaton, "Shall the Commission on Working Harmony Be Abolished?" Only four out of sixteen pages of this edition of *Zion's Advocate* did not deal with the issue of "Working Harmony" relative to building the temple.

[25] Clarence L. Wheaton, "Shall the Commission on Working Harmony Be Abolished?," *Zion's Advocate* 14, no. 6 (June 1937): 217-23.

[26] Ibid., 217-23.

Temple excavation site, late 1930s or early 1940s, BILL CURTIS

Christ should (or should not) solicit arrangements with other factions of the Restoration movement to build the House of the Lord.[27]

In a multi-page article appearing in the November 1937 *Zion's Advocate*, Apostle Leon A. Gould, under the heading of "Awake, Saints, Awake," raised several pertinent points and questions regarding the work on the temple project and then offered several criticisms and suggestions.[28] First, he reviewed the debacle of 1929 and 1930 dealing with Fetting and the associated fallout from that series of events. Second, he recalled the period of fasting and prayer prior to the April 1931 revelation to Apostle Yates, i.e., the need to secure $5000 in the Temple Fund before re-commencing work on the temple. Gould then quoted from the editorial in the July 1931 *Zion's Advocate* wherein the article stated:

> To put a few hundred dollars at a time into the Temple foundation, is to suffer certain loss from the ravages of the elements, that will render a portion of the effort futile; but with five thousand dollars in hand, together with what will most assuredly come in as the work proceeds,

---

[27] Ibid., 211-23.

[28] Leon A. Gould, "Awake, Saints, Awake," *Zion's Advocate* 14, no. 11 (November 1937): 290-92.

the work can be carried to a point that will assure a minimum of loss when winter sets in.[29]

Gould then made this salient observation:

The thousands of dollars that have been expended, a little at a time, with the resultant loss! Indeed, far better would it have been to have postponed work until a sufficient number had proved their willingness to work with the Lord, by taking the first step as he directed.[30]

Next, he presented a financial table that showed the Temple Fund receipts and expenditures by year beginning with funds on hand (as of March 15, 1931) of $388. (This was prior to the Yates revelation requiring $5000 to be in the treasury before a resumption of the work on the temple project could begin). The table ended with a balance in the Temple Fund (as March 15, 1937) of $199. The total receipts for the six-year period were $4498 and the expenses were $4299, not counting voluntary labor and donated equipment and materials.[31] Gould, thereafter, commented:

A total expenditure of better than five thousand dollars, and what have we to show for it? A few thousand feet of rotting lumber, a caving bank, painful memories, and heartache. Can we not learn the lesson of Naaman's healing, of Jericho's fall, of Gideon's victorious army? That obedience means obedience in [the] smallest detail?[32]

Gould next posed the question: "We have tried five thousand dollars' worth of man's way. Are we willing to risk five thousand dollars God's way?" Referring to "Referendum — Bill No. 15" of 1936, he concluded that: "We now have our faces turned in the right direction."[33]

---

[29] Ibid., 290.

[30] Ibid., 290.

[31] Ibid., 292.

[32] Ibid., 292.

[33] Ibid., 292.

To a church member's inquiry: "Why ask us to send any more money for the building of a temple, if it is only to be wasted?" Bishop James R. McClain answered that the money had not been wasted and explained why he felt so.[34] McClain concluded his explanation and pledged that "moneys sent in for the Temple fund" would not be used for any other purpose and added that the "lumber in the yard has been covered so as to protect it from decay until it can be disposed of." His final comment was well chosen in keeping with the future hope of resuming construction on the temple project once the $5000 had been accumulated. It read: "'Fear not little flock,' the Temple will be built by those whom the Lord will approve."[35]

With no resumption of work planned or scheduled until the $5000 had been accumulated in the Temple Fund, little was said or printed regarding the temple project until sometime after the conclusion of the April 1938 conference. On the morning of April 27, 1938, Apostle James E. Yates was seated at a table in his home in Independence, preparing to write a letter to a brother, when he wrote out the question: "Who Shall Build the Temple?" As he pondered an answer to that question he reported that the "Holy Spirit rested upon me" and that "the following message from Our Master was given."[36] The message was lengthy.

It should be remembered that Yates had often taken the position that the temple project should involve all factions of the Restoration and that the Church of Christ should only take the lead. Several verses of this latest revelation specifically pointed to that position. Key excerpts included:

---

[34] Leon A. Gould, "That All May Know," *Zion's Advocate* 14, no. 12 (December 1937): 310.

[35] Ibid., 319.

[36] James E. Yates, "A Spiritual Message (Revelation): To All of the Latter Day Restoration — Independence, Missouri, April 27, 1938;" *Zion's Advocate* 15, no. 7 (July 1938): 106. This article was also printed in pamphlet format.

Not once only have I spoken to my scattered peoples of this Latter Day Dispensation, not twice nor trice only, have I your Lord and Master declared it to be my will that my Temple be built upon the consecrated spot which I have appointed, as hath been known among men and nations. (verse 2)

Yet ye amidst my scattered peoples, who have of means, and who have had wherewith to erect mine House upon the consecrated spot, have devoted your energies to other things. (verse 4)

Yet this once more do I declare that by my spirit in the hearts of all those who truly feel after me, I have been with the various broken fragments of my Church to bless and to comfort, and to shield my people from much of the power of evil. (verse 6)

I call, saith the Lord, upon the broken factions of my spiritual kingdom. Arise ye, arise from your sloth, saith the Holy One, and BUILD YE MINE HOUSE! (verse 9)

Verily, it is I who have [sic] given to the Church of Christ to be custodians of the consecrated lot where my temple shall stand. (verse 10)

I call upon you all amidst my scattered people…all ye of every factional name…Arouse ye! Build my temple in its one and only consecrated place on the Temple lot in the land of Missouri, in the United States of America. (verse 13)

This word I give also specifically to the Church of Christ: boast not [of] yourselves that ye are custodians before the law of the land of my Temple property. Ye can have nothing that is not given you of me. Withhold not yourselves from consultation and prayer with other divisions of my people, when their souls shall hear the call of my spirit to prompt them to consult with you, that all whom I may call, may be permitted to assist in the building of mine House. Fear not to give assurance to those whom I may call to assist in building the Temple, that when the task has been accomplished, their legal rights of interest as brethren in a holy cause, and which their faithful assistance shall have earned, will in righteousness be mutually made secure to all such, before the law of the land; for such justice I shall honor, saith the Lord. (verse 19)

In this task join ye all, whose souls shall hear my call: Build Ye My Temple. (verse 24)[37]

---

[37] Ibid., 106-08. Bold capitalization in the original.

The text of this latest revelation was published in the July 1938 edition of *Zion's Advocate*. In December 1938, Apostle Leon A. Gould analyzed and defended the revelation.[38] He pointed out that the revelation was, in fact, addressed "to all the various factions and divisions of the Restoration, and also in part to the Church of Christ specifically." Gould commented on nearly all of the verses (or paragraphs) and in particular he discussed verse 19.

Regarding verse 19 he remarked that it was specifically directed to the Church of Christ and that the revelation "rebukes boasting, of which we confess too much has been done in the past, and admonishes us to not withhold ourselves from consultation and prayer with other divisions of the Restoration, and with all whom the Lord may call to assist in building the temple. Nothing unreasonable about that, is there?"[39] He then surmised that the objection being expressed was the closing sentence in verse 19 dealing with the counsel "fear not to give assurance to those whom I may call to assist in building the Temple." Gould then concluded: "When considering legal rights, who should own and control, but those who build?...Will someone please arise and tell us who else should be considered?"[40]

Gould's discussion of verse 19, in particular, sounded a lot like the "tabled" report of the "Committee of Working Harmony" which was presented to the assembly at the April 1937 annual conference. Delegates attending that conference were also deeply divided on the issue of "legal rights" should any of the divisions of the "Restoration" step forward to assist.[41]

---

[38] Leon A. Gould, "Revelation and the Temple," *Zion's Advocate* 15, no. 12 (December 1938): 182-85. This article was continued: Leon A. Gould, "Revelation and the Temple," *Zion's Advocate* 16, no. 1 (January 1939): 3-7. The author has referred to each passage as a verse to be consistent with other revelatory material cited herein. In this particular instance Gould has referred to each passage as a paragraph.

[39] Ibid., 184.

[40] Ibid., 185.

[41] "Minutes of the General Ministers Conference of the Church of Christ 1937," *Zion's Advocate* 14, no. 5 (May 1937): 211.

However, the Temple Fund was not forgotten. In the September 1940 *Zion's Advocate*, a "Proclamation and Appeal" was sent out by the Council of Twelve to solicit funds "to accumulate $5000 in the treasury" of the Temple Fund.[42] Also, in the same edition, a "Special Notice" appeared requesting "clothing, old quilts, blankets, etc.," to be sent to "The Temple Builders" in care of Mabel Burns of Detroit, Michigan.[43]

The only other noteworthy action taken in regards to the temple project or the Temple Fund during the next two years by the Church of Christ was the appointment of a committee to "beautify the Temple Lot."[44] This was not an easy task given the size of the "hole" in the middle of the 2¾ acres comprising the Temple Lot. The excavation was 9 feet and 11 inches in depth and 90 feet by 180 feet in width and length.[45] The original assignment to the committee was to specifically level "the dirt taken out of the excavation, and sow grass seed thereon; also to level off the floor of the excavation and seed it; also slope the walls of the same and seed with flowers or running vines."[46] While not an abandonment of the project, it certainly appeared to be a postponement of the church's twelve-year quest to build the House of the Lord.

The committee was also instructed to make an appeal for funds to accomplish the work required. Apostle William A. Anderson, speaking for the committee, stated:

---

[42] Richard B. Trowbridge, "That the People May Know," *Zion's Advocate* 17, no. 9 (September 1940): 137.

[43] Mabel Burns, "The Temple Builders," Zion's Advocate 17, no. 9 (September 1940): 131.

[44] William F. Anderson, "Beautify the Temple Lot," *Zion's Advocate* 17, no. 5 (May 1940): 80.

[45] *Word of the Lord*, 16-20. See verse 2. The "Sixth Message" was received at Fetting's home in Port Huron, Michigan on September 1, 1928.

[46] William F. Anderson, "Beautify the Temple Lot," *Zion's Advocate* 17, no. 5 (May 1940): 80.

We take this means [an article published in *Zion's Advocate*] of asking all who would like to see the grounds terraced and made beautiful. We will appreciate any donations you may wish to send. We do not wish to touch other funds for this work.[47]

This must have been an extremely difficult assignment to accept for those chosen to serve on the committee — and for the majority of the faithful members of the church — given the continual push to donate to the Temple Fund for the past fourteen years.[48] Certainly early collections for this beautification effort conveyed that impression. By August 1940, Rolland Sprague, writing for the Temple Lot Committee, made a specific appeal for help. He stated:

This is neither an easy nor simple matter [the beautification of the Temple Lot]...all should understand that this is general property and that it is not the responsibility of the Independence local church. We hope with a heart sincere that the time will not be long until we will see the Temple being built, but until then we need your help to make this sacred spot more beautiful.[49]

In the two months following the mailing of the October 1940 issue of *Zion's Advocate*, wherein "the plea" of the Council of Twelve Apostles was made, only $1 had been contributed to the Beautifying Temple Lot Fund. As of January 1, 1941, the balance in the Temple Fund stood at $944.[50] During the past year only $326 had been contributed to the fund which included a "return payment of funds formerly loaned out."[51]

---

[47] Ibid.

[48] Clarence L. Wheaton, "Recommendations of the Twelve: April 9th, 1927," *Zion's Advocate* 4, no. 4 (April 1927): 68.

[49] Rolland Sprague, "Temple Lot Committee," *Zion's Advocate* 17, no. 8 (August 1940): 122.

[50] Richard B. Trowbridge, "That the People May Know: General Office Trial Balance," *Zion's Advocate* 18, no. 2 (February 1941): 25

[51] Ibid., 26.

Also noted, and contrary to previously published statements regarding the use of Temple Fund monies for only the temple project, it was admitted that loans had, in fact, been made "out" of the Temple Fund. These loans had been made both to other departments within the church (e.g. to cover a deficit in publishing *Zion's Advocate*) and to certain individuals within the church as well. Trowbridge noted:

> The Auditor's report, as published for last year, shows an item of $595.50 loaned out of the Temple Fund, in addition to what had been paid back. Of this amount we have been able to collect only $62.00[52]

The pleas, proclamations, and sermons of 1941 appear to have had a positive effect on collections for the Temple Fund. Capitalizing on this resurgence in contributions the September 1941, *Zion's Advocate* reprinted the previously issued "Proclamation and Appeal" for contributions to the Temple Fund.[53] The following month a mid-year financial report was issued. The Balance Sheet showed Temple Fund loans due of $533 and a Temple Fund balance of $3282. These figures represented a substantial increase in contributions and loan paybacks.[54]

The office manager, Bishop Richard B. Trowbridge, in issuing the report proudly declared: "The TEMPLE FUND is being fully maintained, and not one cent of it has been 'borrowed' or used for any other purpose than the TRUST FUND."[55] Since assuming the duties of the office manager, Trowbridge had been on a

---

[52] Ibid., 26.

[53] Richard B. Trowbridge, "That the People May Know," *Zion's Advocate* 18, no. 9 (September 1941): 137-8, 143-4. Also cited in *Zion's Advocate* 18, no. 12 (December 1941).

[54] Richard B. Trowbridge, "The Bishops' Forum: Mid-Year Trial Balance Sheet, September 15th, 1941," *Zion's Advocate* 18, no. 10 (October 1941): 153. The mid-year financial report was issued "as of September 15, 1941."

[55] Ibid., 153. Bold Capitalization in the original.

personal mission to "clean up the books." In further discussing the Temple Fund he added:

> Under the old system of 'bookkeeping' where we had no General Ledger, this was not done, causing a very great amount of misunderstanding and trouble. Then, when the 'general funds' were exhausted, Temple Funds had been 'borrowed' for operating purposes and many times the 'loans' had been wiped-out and forgotten at the end of the year. This mistake cannot possibly be made under our new system.[56]

However, the Beautifying Temple Lot Fund carried a balance of less than $7 as shown in the Balance Sheet of September 15, 1941.[57] Perhaps the call for contributions to this "new" fund had had just the opposite effect. Is it possible that the members of the church (as indicated by the dismal figure shown above for the Beautifying Temple Lot Fund) had finally decided to contribute to the Temple Fund and to achieve the required $5000 before they could proceed?

One month later, in November 1941, "The Bishops' Forum," a recently added feature in the monthly *Zion's Advocate*, carried an electrifying report to the membership of the church: "We have gone over the top with our Temple Fund, and that the $5000 has now become a reality, and is no longer just a dream. This news should, we think, cause every member of the Church of Christ to rejoice, and also to take new courage, with a determination to go on with the great work of building the Temple."[58]

Bishop Benjamin A. Winegar, writing for the Bishopric, then posed the rhetorical question: "Who is going to build that Temple?" In answer to his question he remarked:

[56] Ibid., 153.

[57] Ibid., 153.

[58] Benjamin A. Winegar, "The Bishops' Forum," *Zion's Advocate* 18, no. 11 (November 1941): 169.

Did not the Lord say, When you have accumulated the five thousand dollars, then come before me for further instructions? The next step will be just as important as the first one, perhaps more so...

And we are to ask Him what it is, and He will tell us. But unless we are willing to do whatever he tells us to do, it will profit us nothing...

When you recall that since the instruction to accumulate this fund was given, much more than this amount has been expended in a rather fruitless attempt to build the foundation, should we not be very careful now how we proceed? Yes, let us do it God's way — what he tells us to do...

Ever since the beginning of the Restoration there has burned in the hearts of many the hope that they would see the day when the Temple would be built, and a place of refuge established for the saints. In a general way all factions of the restoration believe, and even hope, that they will be permitted to do that work. And we believe that when the time comes that we make ourselves ready, there will be those who are honest in heart who will respond to that divine touch, which will cause them to join in the great work. Let us pray the Lord to hasten the day when this can be.[59]

Obviously, the "hope" to proceed to build the temple had been re-kindled. And, perhaps just as important, the belief that others, within the umbrella of the Restoration, would yet come forward to help the Church of Christ erect the temple.

In further explaining the church's good fortune in "going over the top," Bishop Trowbridge, in the following month's "Bishops' Forum," further explained how "one day, in the regular mail, a very ordinary, innocent little letter came to his desk. On opening it can you imagine his surprise and very great joy to have a perfectly good check for $1912.50 drop out of this letter — to be used as Temple Funds?"[60]

Trowbridge, who authorized the article, also remarked that after the 1940 "Proclamation and Appeal" had been issued and the positive response to it, "almost immediately the effort was

[59] Ibid., 169-70.

[60] Richard B. Trowbridge, "The Bishops' Forum," *Zion's Advocate* 18, no. 12 (December 1941): 185.

met by a very decided opposition, even by some who had joined in the extending of this approval." He further commented that with the announcement and the "wonderful boost to the Temple Fund, however, there also came from opposition forces some very caustic, unfair critisisms [sic] about how the raising [of] the Temple Fund was 'freezing up the income of the Church.'"[61]

However, within only four months, the April 1942 issue of *Zion's Advocate* reported that $4000 had been "withdrawn" from the Temple Fund and placed elsewhere for "safe keeping."[62] Meanwhile, Trowbridge completed, on April 2, 1942, the "Annual Financial Statement of Books" for the year ended March 15, 1942. The printing of the statement occurred just prior to the opening of the April 1942 annual conference of the church.[63] To the "Statement of Books" he added an "Addenda" which explained, in summary (from Trowbridge's perspective), the significant events and adjustments to the church's financial status for the past year.[64]

A combination of zeal and frustration was evident in his narrative. In referring to the temple, Trowbridge commented that it was "sad, sad indeed to see the sacred place designated and dedicated for the VERY important need of the building of God's Holy Temple...lying waste, idle, forsaken, abandoned, while many who pretend to be God's children, are still very unconcerned and indifferent, and are yet yielding themselves and their substance to the unprofitable, idle worship of Baal and Babylon."[65]

---

[61] Ibid.

[62] Richard B. Trowbridge, "Of General Interest: Annual Financial Statement of Books and Addenda," *Zion's Advocate* 19, no. 4 (April 1942): 55.

[63] Ibid., 54-6. It is apparent that either the April issue of *Zion's Advocate* was available prior to the commencement of the annual conference or the "financial report and detail" was printed separately and made available to members prior to the beginning of the first business session of the April conference.

[64] Ibid., 55-6.

[65] Ibid., 55. Bold capitalization in original.

He then discussed the situation relative to the Temple Fund. While noting that tithes and offerings had doubled from the previous year, contributions to the "Temple Fund have been increased ONLY by about Four Hundred Dollars...owing to the unwise and unfair propaganda that has been urged against this important work and the manifest disposition on the part of some to divert all funds to other purposes."[66]

Trowbridge further explained:

> I feel sure that the membership of the Church will feel sad and very much disappointed to learn that the Temple Fund, which was about $5,600.00, has been 'set back' by the temporary withdrawal from that fund of about Four Thousand Dollars, which was pledged and given under the promises as set out in the Temple Fund pledges, which we sent out. This action was taken solely because of the strange actions and unwise conduct of some high in authority. However, the amount is NOT entirely 'lost to the Temple Fund,' but is simply 'withdrawn' and is being held in reserve and 'in trust' for safekeeping for the fund, until such time as it is needed for actual Temple building, so that really and truly the available Temple Fund is still about Fifty-six Hundred Dollars."[67]

All did not go well for Bishop Trowbridge at the annual April (1942) conference of the church. His aggressive and pre-published explanation relative to the "temporary" withdrawal of $4000 from the Temple Fund was fodder for extended and heated debate.[68] In fact, the June 1942 edition of *Zion's Advocate* was totally dedicated to the issues raised and discussed at the April conference. Apostle Bert C. Flint, editor of the church newspaper *Zion's Advocate*, introduced a special "Editorial" with the statement: "Because of the crisis through which we are now passing, it seemed advisable to withhold our regular Editorial."[69]

---

[66] Ibid., 55. Bold capitalization in original.

[67] Ibid., 55. Bold capitalization in original.

[68] Arthur M. Smith, "To the Church of Christ and All the Readers of the Advocate," *Zion's Advocate* 19, no. 5 (May 1942): 68.

[69] Bert C. Flint, "From the Editor," *Zion's Advocate* 19, no. 6 (June 1942): 82.

The article which followed Flint's remarks was written by Apostle Arthur M. Smith. It was a lengthy piece dealing with the "crisis" to which Flint had already alluded. Smith also noted that this issue had occupied the majority of the time spent by the delegates at the recently ended April conference.[70]

The "crisis" was referred to as the "Trowbridge situation." Bishop Richard B. Trowbridge was asked to explain, in detail, the entries in the annual "Statement of Books" published on April 2, 1942. His explanation was found unsatisfactory. Trowbridge was forced to switch from explaining his actions to justifying his actions. His defense was to continually question and challenge the actions of other church leaders. And, of significant importance, he would not provide further explanation regarding the whereabouts of the $4000 which had been "temporarily withdrawn."[71]

Apostle Smith compared the current situation to that faced by the church in 1929 just prior to and following Otto Fetting's departure from the church. He stated: "We now are face to face with an almost identical situation." Smith further explained that the recent conference had "appointed a committee to obtain an audit of the books, (in order to relieve the rejected business manger — Bishop Richard B. Trowbridge)," etc. The committee, he stated, had "met with very stern opposition and it again became necessary to appeal to the courts of the land." The initial decision of "Circuit Judge Waltner" was to appoint a temporary receiver for the church.[72] Smith continued:

> Still the tragedy of it is not complete; because once again funds have been withdrawn from the bank, in large amounts, and the church knows nothing of its whereabouts, nor can the Committee intrusted [sic] with this matter find out. And, added to this there are bills and

[70] Arthur M. Smith, "History Repeats Itself," *Zion's Advocate* 19, no. 6 (June 1942): 82-3.

[71] "General Conference Minutes: Independence, Missouri [1942]," *Zion's Advocate* 19, no. 6 (June 1942): 84-100.

[72] Arthur M. Smith, "History Repeats Itself," *Zion's Advocate* 19, no. 6 (June 1942): 82.

obligations that amount to more than the balance left in the General Funds. So again, "history repeats itself."[73]

The June 1942 publication of *Zion's Advocate* included an "outside" auditor's report of the church funds (a Kansas City, Missouri, CPA firm had been hired). In the "Comments" section of the report, Roy A. Guyton, CPA, noted that on September 30, 1941, Bishop Richard B. Trowbridge drew a check on the "General Bank Account payable" to himself as Bishop and Trustee for the Temple Fund in the sum of $5,298.21 and deposited [it] to the Temple Fund Bank Account on the same day in the name of the Church of Christ with Bishop Trowbridge as Trustee."[74]

Guyton further explained that on the same day "a certified check payable to Mrs. T. Alice Bender for $3,912.50 was charged to the Temple Fund Bank Account. I noticed that during this year this same person had contributed large funds for the Temple, but I found no evidence that the amount withdrawn had been redeposited in another special Temple Fund of the Church." In fact, Mrs. Bender had recently donated $1912.50. The receipt of her check had prompted Trowbridge, as previously stated, to announce that the Temple Fund had finally gone over the $5000 requirement. The balance of the cash on deposit in the Temple Fund bank account (after the Guyton audit) at March 15, 1942 was $1,626.98.[75]

[73] Ibid.

[74] Roy A. Guyton, C.P.A., "Roy A. Guyton & Company, Certified and Public Accountants, Kansas City, Missouri, May 6th, 1942," *Zion's Advocate* 19, no. 6 (June 1942): 83-7.

[75] Ibid., 85.

Efforts Curtailed: 1943–1946

I N THE MIDST of the internal troubles at the Church of Christ over the whereabouts of the Temple Fund and the court action involving Bishop Richard B. Trowbridge, another request to help "beautify the Temple Lot" was issued in June 1942.[1] Minutes of the April 1942 church conference noted that the committee which had been appointed two years previous to "beautify the Temple Lot…and to tear down the 'care-taker's' cabin on the back of the lot"[2] had failed "to function."[3] Perhaps the reason for the committee's failure was that only $6.88 had been contributed to the Beautifying Temple Lot Fund.

A new motion was made and voted upon that a new "committee of three be appointed to investigate the probable cost…of the fixing of this property on the back of the Temple Lot." The new committee reported that afternoon: "We do not advise remodeling this building because of conditions" but "that the present building should not be wrecked until work is ready to start on the new building" (a prefabricated building to replace the existing structure).[4]

As yet, however, the church had not abandoned their quest to build a temple on that sacred space of 2¾ acres known as the

---

[1] "General Conference Minutes: Independence, Missouri [1942]," *Zion's Advocate* 19, no. 6 (June 1942): 94.

[2] William F. Anderson, "Beautify the Temple Lot," *Zion's Advocate* 17, no. 5 (May 1940): 80.

[3] "General Conference Minutes: Independence, Missouri [1942]," *Zion's Advocate* 19, no. 6 (June 1942): 94.

[4] Ibid.

Temple Lot. In an update to the *Articles of Faith and Practice of the Church of Christ* (printed in May 1942), their belief was again made clear in Article number 22. The article begins with the emphatic statement:

> We believe a temple will be built in this generation, in Independence, Missouri, wherein Christ will reveal himself and endow his servants whom he chooses with power to preach the gospel in all the world to every kindred, tongue, and people, that the promise of God to Israel be fulfilled.[5]

In an article prepared by Apostle James E. Yates for the February 1943 edition of *Zion's Advocate*, he stated:

> Even though some of our people should become discouraged and lose faith in the revelations that have been given declaring that the Temple of the Lord will be built on the designated Temple Lot in Independence, Missouri, the greater number of our Latter Day Saint people will maintain their faith, and THAT TEMPLE WILL BE BUILT![6]

He added, however:

> But until the people, who should erect this Temple to the honor of the great name of our living Master, can learn to put *applied Christianity* ahead of *selfish Churchianity* the Temple Building program can not go forward acceptably to Him.[7]

Yates' statement that there was a serious "but until" regarding the "Temple Building program," reflected a significant change to the previous writings and sermons of Apostle Yates. While he did not back away from the revelations previously proclaimed through him in the 1930s, or his position regarding the "other

---

[5] "Articles of Faith and Practice of the Church of Christ (Temple Lot)," *Zion's Advocate* 19, no. 5 (May 1942): 67-8.

[6] James E. Yates, "The Crystal Fountain of Life: Prayerfully Dedicated to All Latter Day Saint People," *Zion's Advocate* 20, no. 2 (February 1943): 30. Bold capitalization in original.

[7] Ibid., 30. Note: Bold print and Capitalization in original.

Aerial view of the temple property showing RLDS Stone Church, Church of Christ (Temple Lot) chapel, and RLDS Church Auditorium, COMMUNITY OF CHRIST LIBRARY-ARCHIVES

factions" of the "Restoration" coming forth to help build the temple, his concluding comment in the February 1943 article cited above was certainly an indication that his ardent position of building the temple "now" had been modified. The members of the Church of Christ had been through so much turmoil in their hopes, desires, and expectations to build the House of the Lord for 15 years, that the missing $4000 from the Temple Fund, had finally taken its toll, even on Apostle Yates.

In February 1943 the Jackson County Circuit Court "Receiver's Final Report and Application for Final Discharge" in the matter of Barton, Bell and Yates as Trustees for the Church of Christ versus Richard B. Trowbridge, Defendant, was issued.[8]

---

[8] "In the Circuit Court of Jackson County, Missouri, At Independence, December Term 1942, Thomas E. Barton, Archie Bell and Joseph [James] E. Yates, as Trustees for, Church of Christ, (Temple Lot) an Unincorporated Religious Organization[,]

The report recapped the appointment of Walter B. Davis, Receiver, and his ordering of "a fiscal audit of the finances of the said Church of Christ by Mr. Roy A. Guyton, a certified public accountant." Davis noted that the audit was updated to February 1, 1943, and, among other items, noted that Temple Fund account balance was $1,661.48. He also acknowledged: (1) that the removal of the office manager (Richard B. Trowbridge) had been accomplished; (2) that "a special conference of the Church of Christ," as ordered by the court, had been held November 16–18, 1942, "for the purpose of rehabilitating the Bishopric" and in selecting a new office manager; and, finally, (3) that a vote had been taken and "a new manager...chosen."[9]

At the April 12, 1943, afternoon session of the annual conference, it was moved by Apostle Thomas J. Jordan that "we abolish both the Plans and Temple Building Committees and that we refer the building of the Temple to the General Bishopric and that we instruct the General Bishopric to proceed with the building of the Temple as soon as sufficient funds and material are in hand without debt to the Church."[10] Two days later, the motion was amended by adding "plans and material on hand be placed in the hands of the General Bishopric." The motion to amend was voted upon and carried.[11] The Temple Fund, in trust, was reported by the auditor to be $1661.[12]

With the realities of World War II very much on the minds of the members of the Church of Christ, and, in particular, the need for gasoline rationing, the annual conference for 1944 was

---

Plaintiffs vs. Richard B. Trowbridge, Defendant: Receiver's Final Report and Application for Final Discharge," *Zion's Advocate* 20, no. 4 (April 1943): 52-3.

[9] Ibid., 52-3. The new business manager, Walter B. Davis, was the court appointed "Receiver," and a member of the Church of Christ.

[10] "Minutes of the Ministers' Conference of the Church of Christ (Temple Lot) Convened April 6, 1943 on the Temple Lot," *Zion's Advocate* 20, no. 5 (May 1943): 74.

[11] Ibid., 81.

[12] Ibid., 82.

Marker commemorating the Temple Site, ALEX BAUGH

cancelled.[13] Between 1943 and 1946 any attempts to discuss or re-visit the previous efforts of the church to beautify the Temple Lot appear to have been dismissed or ignored. In the interim, the excavation site continued to deteriorate and became overgrown with weeds and, apparently, an eyesore and a potential safety hazard to the citizens of Independence.

At the 1946 April conference, a motion was presented to "now take up the matter of filling in the excavation on the Temple Lot."[14] Apparently, an "offer" had been presented by the City of Independence to officials of the Church of Christ, wherein the city had indicated that it would "fill-in" the excavation site at city expense.[15] The motion to accept the city's offer was unanimous.

---

[13] Arthur M. Smith, Bert C. Flint, and James E. Yates, "Action of the Quorum of Twelve: Independence, Missouri, October 7, 1943," *Zion's Advocate* 20, no. 12 (December 1943): 185.

[14] "Minutes of Ministers' Conference, 1946," *Zion's Advocate* 23, no. 5 (May 1946): 70-1.

[15] Ibid., 71. The motion stated: "That we accept the offer of the city to fill the excavation."

A committee was then appointed at the conference to call upon the City Planning Commission to "accept their offer to grade the excavation for the Temple, and to work with the City in a supervisory capacity over this work."[16]

The City of Independence, after being advised by the church of their unanimous agreement, back-filled the excavation site for the temple (begun in 1929 and mostly completed by 1933–34) as promised. For nearly 17 years the "spot for the temple" (LDS D&C 57:3 and RLDS D&C 57:1.d.) had stood as a constant reminder to the membership of the Christ of Christ of their efforts and sacrifices, as well as their frustrations and disappointments, of their quest to build the House of the Lord. At a meeting of the church, held in April 1947, Apostle Clarence L. Wheaton reported: "that the excavation had been filled, grass seed planted, and trees trimmed."[17]

[16] Ibid.

[17] "General Conference Minutes: Independence, Missouri [1947]," *Zion's Advocate* 24, no. 5 (May 1947).

But the Temple was Not Forgotten

T HE APRIL 1948 conference, having moved past the "fill-in" of the excavation site presented *A Handbook of Conference Resolutions and Enactments* to the church for a referendum vote. As part of the *"Handbook,"* a slightly revised "Articles of Faith and Practice" was included. In spite of all the misgivings of the past seventeen years, Article number 23 (previously known as number 22) again reiterated that "a temple will be built in this generation, in Independence."[1]

View to north showing Church of Christ (Temple Lot) 1992 chapel and in-ground marker placed by Missouri Mormon Frontier Foundation, ALEX BAUGH

[1] "Bills for 1948: Notice to All Branches and Members," *Zion's Advocate* 25, no. 5 (Supplement) (May 1948): Referendum, 3-5.

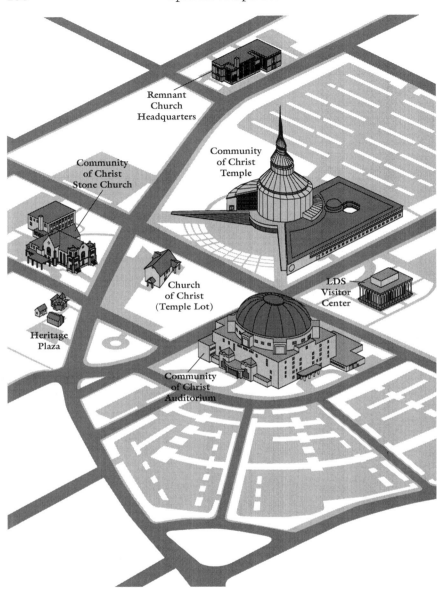

A diagram showing the Temple Lot today, JOHN HAMER

Conclusion

IN THE YEARS that followed the "filling-in" of the excavation site and the Beautifying of the Temple Lot Fund Drive, the desire to build a temple faded. However, certain of the Church of Christ's Council of Twelve occasionally voiced themselves regarding their belief of the eventual erection of "the Temple" on that sacred space known as the Temple Lot. This was particularly true for those who had been a part of the exciting, yet disappointing, period of church history dealing with the temple project. Certainly one of those who had seen "first-hand" the turbulent period from 1926 to 1946 was Apostle Clarence L. Wheaton.

In 1969, Apostle Wheaton met with President Alvin R. Dyer, counselor in the First Presidency of the Church of Jesus Christ of Latter-day Saints. Wheaton recalled that when the two of them stood before the "Marker on the Temple Lot, President Dyer said 'the House of the Lord will be built on this spot, which you people own.'" Dyer further elaborated:

> Under these circumstances it behooves each and every person who loves the work of the Restoration of these last days, regardless to which division they belong, to come forward with their means, their prayers, and moral and spiritual support to see that this great work is begun.[1]

---

[1] Clarence L. Wheaton, Sermon, circa 1970, 6. Sermon was delivered (n.d.) in Independence, Missouri. This is an eight-page double-spaced typewritten document. The message of the sermon deals with plans for the temple that the Church of Christ contemplated building, beginning in 1929. Photocopy in possession of the author.

Thirty years later, Bishop C. Andrew Brantner wrote an excellent article for the August 1999 issue of *Zion's Advocate* titled: "The Generation of the Gathering."[2] Bishop Brantner wrote of the early revelations of the Prophet Joseph Smith as they related to the "City of the New Jerusalem" and the "Temple in Zion." He referenced "temple related" scriptures in both the Bible and the Book of Mormon. Brantner recalled the revelation to Granville Hedrick in 1864 and the return of his followers to Jackson County to reclaim the Temple Lot. Brantner quoted "Article number 23" from the church's *Articles of Faith and Practice*[3] which resolutely declared again, that "a temple will be built in this generation, in Independence, Missouri." He then asked his readers the rhetorical question:

> In what generation? Why the generation of the gathering! This is the whole purpose of the Restoration to restore the House of Israel to a oneness with each other, and most importantly, with God.[4]

The Temple Lot, as it is referred to by all divisions or schisms of the Restoration movement, was the driving force, as mentioned by Bishop Brantner, for Granville Hedrick's followers in and around central Illinois, to sell their farms, businesses, and homes and travel to Independence, Jackson County, Missouri, beginning in the winter of early 1867. Between 1867 and 1874 John H. Hedrick (Granville Hedrick's brother) and William Eaton proceeded to re-purchase the eight contiguous lots at, and immediately adjacent to, the "spot for the temple lying westward, upon a lot which is not far from the courthouse" (LDS D&C 57:1-4; RLDS D&C 57:1-2). In doing so, the Center Place of Zion was saved and preserved. Furthermore, this acquisition prompted serious attention by the RLDS and

---

[2] C. Andrew Brantner, "The Generation of the Gathering," *Zion's Advocate* 76, no. 8 (August 1999): 125-32.

[3] *Articles of Faith and Practice* (Independence, Missouri: Board of Publications, Church of Christ, 1970), 6.

[4] C. Andrew Brantner, "The Generation of the Gathering," *Zion's Advocate* 76, no. 8 (August 1999): 132.

Aerial view to east-southeast showing Church of Christ (Temple Lot)
meetinghouse and surrounding properties owned by other Restoration churches,
LDS Intellectual Reserve

LDS Churches in subsequent years to acquire the remainder of the 63.27 acres purchased by Edward Partridge for the original church in December 1831.[5]

In retrospect, some might conclude that the notion of building a magnificent temple, as envisioned by the Fetting "Messages" of 1927–1929, was too much of an undertaking for this numerically small but determined group of adherents to the early revelations of Joseph Smith Jr. Given their membership base and economic status in 1929, the temple project, as contemplated, was formidable. The members of the Church of Christ, however, did not look at the task "being asked of them" as impossible. They truly believed that the Lord would, somehow, provide.

The Church of Christ attempted, on several occasions, to include other divisions of the Restoration in their efforts to build "the Temple." These efforts to raise the needed money and/or

---

[5] Jackson County, Property Records, B:1, Independence, Missouri. The exact date of the purchase is noted in the records: "Jones H. Flourney and Clara, his wife...to Edward Partridge, 63 and 43/160th acres in Section 3, Township 9, Range 32...dated December 19, 1831."

to solicit participation in some other way proved fruitless. Their own efforts to fund the project as a church body were adversely impacted by the economic realities of the Great Depression, their limited membership base, schism with the church, and failure to generate support from other divisions of the Restoration. The Church of Christ added to their own fund raising problems, however, with diversionary solicitations to invest in oil drilling in Canada, gold mining in the mountains of the West, and a cooperative farming project in Missouri. How much was invested in these ventures is unknown. It is doubtful that any significant amount of discretionary funds would have had much of an impact given the scope of the church's enormous undertaking.

The relative lack of money with which to build "the Temple," coupled with internal difficulties that began with Apostle Otto Fetting and ended with Bishop Richard B. Trowbridge, placed the church in an untenable position. In the end, the financial pressures of the Depression, followed by the constraints of World War II, were, simply, too much. Yet, in spite of a never-ending string of difficulties and demands, one cannot but admire the members of the Church of Christ for their extraordinary faith and devotion. Throughout sixteen years (1927–1943) of excitement, anxiety, and frustration, they, as a church, diligently tried to get "the Temple" built as they believed they had been divinely directed to do.

Currently, the Church of Christ has no plans for the physical construction of the House of the Lord, even though the church does continue to maintain a Temple Fund. In the years that followed 1943 (when the Plans and Temple Building Committees were abolished), the temple project was relegated to a low priority by the leadership of the church. Today the temple project is not considered a "primary focus" of the church.[6]

---

[6] Apostle William A. Sheldon, Church of Christ, Interviewed by R. Jean Addams, April 2006. Sheldon, email to Addams, December 2006, confirmed, after reaffirming that the building of "the Temple" was not a core objective of the church, stated: "the primary focus [of the church] is missionary work and building up the Kingdom of God." Referring again to the temple project, he added: "We will simply await the Lord's further direction."

Index

About the Author

R. JEAN ADDAMS is a lifetime Mormon History enthusiast and independent historian. He and his wife Liz reside in Woodinville, Washington.

He holds a BS in Accounting and an MBA from the University of Utah and recently retired as a Vice President and CFO for a corporation in the Seattle area. Addams has written, presented, and had published several articles dealing with the Church of Christ (Temple Lot). He is the author of "Reclaiming the Temple Lot in the Center Place of Zion," *Mormon Historical Studies* 7 (Spring/Fall 2006); "The Church of Christ (Temple Lot), Its Emergence, Struggles and Early Schisms," in *Scattering of the Saints: Schism within Mormonism*, edited by Newell G. Bringhurst and John C. Hamer (Independence: John Whitmer Books, 2007); "The Church of Christ (Temple Lot) and the Law of Consecration," *John Whitmer Historical Association Journal* 28 (2008); with Alexander L. Baugh, "'Upon a Lot...Not Far from the Courthouse': A Photographic History of the Temple Lot in Independence, Jackson County, Missouri," *Mormon Historical Studies* 9, no. 2 (Fall 2008); "The Church of Christ (Temple Lot) and the Reorganized Church of Jesus Christ of Latter Day Saints: 130 Years of Crossroads and Controversies," *Journal of Mormon History* 36, no. 2 (Spring 2010); and "Early Sociological Issues Confronted by the Church of Christ (Temple Lot): African Americans, Native Americans, and Women," *John Whitmer Historical Association Journal* 30 (2010).

His interests include family, skiing, and fishing.